The Impact of Work Schedules
on the Family

The Impact of Work Schedules on the Family

Graham L. Staines
Joseph H. Pleck

with a foreword by
Urie Bronfenbrenner

Survey Research Center • Institute for Social Research
The University of Michigan

1983

The preparation of this monograph has been supported by Grant No. 90–C–1774 from the federal Administration of Children, Youth and Families.

Library of Congress Cataloging in Publication Data:

Staines, Graham L.
  The impact of work schedules on the family.

  Bibliography: p.
  1. Family — United States.   2. Hours of labor — United
States.   3. Hours of labor, Flexible — United States.
4. Social surveys — United States.   5. Married people —
Employment — Social aspects — United States.   I. Pleck,
Joseph H.   II. Title.
HQ536.S72   1983   306.8′5   83–8451
ISBN 0–87944–284–0

ISR Code Number 4550

Published in 1983 by:
The Institute for Social Research
The University of Michigan, Ann Arbor, Michigan

6 5 4 3 2
Manufactured in the United States of America

About the Authors

GRAHAM L. STAINES, formerly a study director with the Organizational Behavior Program of the Survey Research Center at the Institute for Social Research, is now Assistant Professor of Psychology at Rutgers University.

JOSEPH H. PLECK, formerly a study director with the Family and Sex Roles Program of the Survey Research Center at the Institute for Social Research, is now a program director with the Center for Research on Women at Wellesley College.

Acknowledgements

We wish to express our appreciation to both the institutions which supported and the individuals who contributed to the preparation of this book. Funding for the study came from the federal Administration for Children, Youth and Families under grant number 90–C–1774. Our project officers at the Administration, Aeolian Jackson and Maiso Bryant, were unfailingly courteous and helpful during all phases of the investigation. Our three research assistants, Pamela O'Connor, David Pagnucco, and Michael Rustad, made many excellent contributions to the project, especially in their efficient handling of the data processing. We are also grateful to Robert P. Quinn, who assisted generously in the preparation of the research proposal, to Bernard Goitein and James S. House, who kindly discussed a variety of difficult methodological issues with us, and to the reviewers at the Institute for Social Research, who read an early draft of the manuscript. Finally, we wish to thank Libby Brusca, Harriet Cohen, Pat Fusco, and Marguerite Rupp, who provided us with able clerical assistance during the typing of the manuscript, and Aimée Ergas and the staff of the Publishing Division of the Institute for Social Research, who edited the manuscript and prepared it for publication.

Foreword

In this volume, Graham Staines and Joseph Pleck report the results of the first *systematic* study of the effect of work schedules on family stress. I use the word "systematic" deliberately. The previous studies in this area, all of which are summarized in this work, typically conceptualized both work schedules and psychological stress in single variable terms and then examined the association between pairs of variables, one from each setting, taking one pair at a time. Staines and Pleck see both the world of work and the family as more complex, and they manage to capture this complexity by employing methods that are at once sophisticated and sensible. Thus, in analyzing work schedules, they distinguish four aspects of the phenomenon: the pattern of days worked each week, the pattern of hours worked each day, the number of hours worked each week, and the flexibility of work schedule. Each aspect is examined for its separate impact, and their joint effects are analyzed as well. Similar attention is shown to patterns with respect to outcomes. The investigators relate information about behavior (time spent on child care and housework) to psychological state (perception of interference between work and family life, degree of perceived family conflict). They then proceed to examine not only the relationships between patterns in one domain and patterns in the other, but also how the relationships are moderated by other factors, for example the degree of control that each person has over his or her own work schedule.

The most important "systems property" investigated in this research is the combined effect of both parents' work schedules on the family life of each. Although attention to such interdependence has been urged in recent research reviews of the area (Bronfenbrenner and Crouter, 1982; Hoffman, 1980; ibid, 1983), this is the first time that it has been incorporated into the research design.

All these innovations are given added significance by their application to a large national sample (2,850 households) reflecting the actual distribution of various types of work schedules in the population.

The quality of the research design in this study is reflected in the quality of its findings, which serve both to confirm previously suspected effects and to record previously undocumented trends. In the former sphere, perhaps the clearest and most important finding is that an irregular pattern of working days (weekend work, variable schedules during the week) has a negative impact on the quality of family life, as reflected in reduced time spent in family activities, higher levels of perceived work/family interference, and problems in family adjustment. Husbands are much more likely than wives to be working such irregular schedules. Indeed, even though the majority of mothers in the U.S. are now working, Staines and Pleck have found that, compared to employed men, employed women average twice as much time with their children and two and one half times as much on housework. Other aspects of work schedules also influence family stress in similar fashion, but to lesser degree. For example, both the number of hours worked and shiftwork are associated with more job/family conflict, but neither has any significant effect on the number of hours spent in child care.

Far more important than the overall effect of these temporal arrangements is the moderating influence of the degree of control that a person has over his or her work schedule. Of the several potential mediating factors examined (such as educational level, stage in the family life cycle, and type of working arrangements in the family), this is the only factor to exhibit a consistent effect. That is, in line with the authors' hypothesis, some measure of control over one's work schedule tends to reduce the negative impact of irregular and excessive working hours.

Finally, in the previously unexplored area of the joint effects of both parents' work schedules, the analyses reveal both expected multiplicative effects and some intriguing asymmetries. For example, a wife's schedule conflicts are exacerbated when her husband works weekends, whereas his conflicts are enhanced when she works an irregular shift during the week.

Clearly Staines and Pleck's research has added new knowledge and new understanding of the psychological effects of a major change taking place in modern American society. Yet, this is not the most important contribution of their work; that is still to come. By employing elegant designs that can reveal more effectively the impact of work schedules and arrangements on family stress, they have set the stage for the next phases of inquiry. For example, to what extent can the stressful effects of problematic work schedules be ameliorated by introducing personnel policies that increase the employee's control over his or her working hours? And when such stress does occur, to what degree does it influence actual behavior with respect to performance on the job or patterns of parent-child interaction in the home? Finally, do such behavioral changes, in turn, affect the future course of development not only of children but of parents themselves? The work of Staines and Pleck is making its most important contribution to the development of both science and social policy by providing us with new and better methods and ideas for pursuing these issues.

Urie Bronfenbrenner
Cornell University

References

Bronfenbrenner, U., and Crouter, A.C. "Work and family through time and space." In *Families that work: Children in a changing world*, edited by S. Kamerman and C.D. Hayes. Washington, DC: National Academy Press, 1982.

Hoffman, L.W. "Work, family and the socialization of the child." In *Review of Child Development Research, Vol. 7: The Family*, edited by R.D. Park. Chicago: University of Chicago Press, 1983.

Contents

List of Tables

1

Introduction

Work Life vs. Family Life

In recent years, there has been an upsurge of interest in the impact of work on the family. Scholars such as Kanter (1977) have observed that although the social sciences have traditionally studied occupations and the family in isolation, each in fact influences the other in a variety of ways that deserve research attention. The 1981 White House Conference on Families included as one of its major policy recommendations that employers institute more family-oriented personnel policies. It is now becoming almost commonplace to talk about the "work/family interface."

Among all the ways that work and family life affect each other, the impact of work schedules on family life has emerged as a topic of special concern. There have, of course, been numerous earlier investigations of other effects of work schedules, particularly the health consequences of shiftwork and the effects of flextime, the four-day workweek, and part-time work on productivity. Complementing these earlier studies, a new line of research has more recently focused on the impacts of such nontraditional or innovative schedule patterns, as well as on variations in number of hours worked per week and other fundamental schedule variables, specifically on workers' family lives. In contrast to other aspects of work that affect the family, such as pay, social relations in the workplace, and unemployment, the scheduling of work hours seems particularly accessible to policy intervention.

Recent increases in wives' rates of employment in particular have stimulated interest in interrelationships between work schedules and families. Both popular and professional observers recognize that many of the issues involved in "wives' employment" — perhaps the social hallmark of our era — are issues about the scheduling of paid jobs to take into account child rearing and other family responsibilities. Increasingly, experiments and innovations in work schedules are being proposed and implemented to effectively relieve work/family conflicts, particularly for the current majority of two-earner couples. To a large extent, the beneficial effects on the family of alternative patterns of work schedules have been conceptualized as occurring primarily among employed wives and mothers. Now, some observers are noting as well the potential of alternative work schedules to relieve *men's* work/family conflicts and to facilitate men's integration of their paid work and family roles (Pleck, in press).

This volume describes the results of a study of the impact of work schedules on family life.[1] It classifies work schedules according to four general dimensions applicable to all schedules: pattern of days worked each week, pattern of hours worked each day, number of hours worked each week, and flexibility of work schedules. These four dimensions capture some but not all of the issues raised by the better publicized but less frequent special schedules, such as flextime and the four-day week. The study extends its dimensional approach into the measurement of the quality of family life. Specifically, it assesses family life in terms of: (1) the amount of time spent in carrying out the family responsibilities of child care and housework, (2) reports of interference between work and family life, and (3) levels of family adjustment.

Chapter 2 presents our approach to and hypotheses about the critical dimensions of work schedules and family life examined in our study. It also reviews some of the current general trends in work and family life in our society and looks at the findings of past research on how dimensions of work schedules influence the family. Chapter 3 describes the survey sample, the questionnaire, and other technical aspects of the study. Chapter 4 presents our findings on the impact of the patterns of days and hours and number of hours worked on time spent in family roles, on work/family conflict, and on family adjustment. Chapter 5 examines how the worker's degree of control over his or her schedule influences the degree and kind of impact that schedule has on the worker's family life. Chapter 6 presents a variety of special analyses of schedule/family relationships in the emerging majority of two-earner couples. Finally, Chapter 7 concludes with a general summary and interpretation of our results and the implications for future research and policy making.

An Overview of the Study

This study attempts to illuminate the nature, characteristics, and consequences of contemporary patterns of work schedules on family life. It does so through detailed analyses of reports by a national sample of workers concerning their job schedules and family life, collected in the 1977 Quality of Employment Survey conducted by the Survey Research Center at the Institute for Social Research. Although many studies of the relationship between work schedules and family life omit employed women from their samples, this study does not. By including an appropriate proportion of working women in the sample, it gives proper emphasis to dual-earner families and to families headed by women.

The study generates three major empirical findings. First, certain kinds of job schedules appear to have a negative influence on workers' family lives. Offending schedules include nonstandard patterns of days each week (e.g., weekend work, variable patterns of days), nonstandard patterns of hours each day (e.g., shiftwork), and working a large number of hours each week.

Second, such potentially stressful job schedules appear to have the most negative effects on workers who have the least control over their schedules. Among workers who have high schedule control, the impact on family life of weekend work, shiftwork, and excessive weekly hours seems to be less detrimental.

Third, the apparent effects of one spouse's job schedule go beyond that individual's own family life and extend to the other spouse's job schedule and family life. One spouse's schedule can influence the schedule that the other spouse works. One spouse's stressful job schedule can reduce the quality of the other spouse's family life, and it can intensify the relationship between the other spouse's job schedule and family life.

Our empirical findings have important policy implications because the impact of work schedules on family life appears likely to become a salient social issue in the foreseeable future. Of particular importance to policy makers are the implications of the findings from our analysis of schedule control as a moderator variable. Most existing research has limited the investigation of workers' schedule control to an evaluation of flextime schedules. As a consequence, such research has interpreted schedule control only as the flexibility of the starting and ending time of a day's work and has searched for only the main effects of flexibility on the quality of family life. By comparison, our research points to a variety of components of schedule flexibility: control over days worked and hours worked, the ability to get time off during the workday to take care of personal business, and the degree of schedule variability allowed on a day-to-day or week-to-week basis. Serious issues of practicality arise, of course, if workers enjoy wide latitude in their schedules, but the important point is that a variety of dimensions of schedule control may have positive implications for family life. The current research also underscores the importance of not judging the contribution of schedule control to the quality of family life merely in terms of its main effects. Policy makers need to recognize that schedule control may have major implications for families because it can moderate the relationships between work schedule characteristics and family life.

The analyses of the work schedules of dual-earner couples raise a second set of policy issues. When both spouses work, one spouse's work schedule can have both direct (main) and indirect (moderator) effects on the other spouse's family life. If policy decisions about work schedules are to take into account the known relationships between schedules and family life, the schedules of husbands and wives in dual-earner couples deserve joint consideration.

Our conclusions and the results of our analyses should be of interest to employment policy makers, those concerned with alternative work schedules, and the personnel and employee relations units of firms and organizations.

Note

1. The present report supercedes several earlier analyses of the same dataset, which are not included in the ensuing review of literature. It supercedes, for example, earlier reports on the frequency of work/family conflict among different demographic subgroups and on the bivariate correlates of work/family conflict, including various measures of work schedules (Pleck et al., 1978; ibid, 1980). The present report also supercedes an analysis of the patterns of time use and levels of family adjustment reported by employed wives and two subgroups of employed husbands (Pleck and Lang, 1978).

2

The Present Study in Context

Introduction

Previous investigations of the relationship between work and family life have examined various dimensions of each concept, but certain combinations of dimensions of work and family life have remained largely unexplored. Like its predecessors, this study confines itself to a limited number of dimensions of work and family life. In the case of work, it focuses exclusively on work schedules, leaving to other studies the task of investigating such factors as occupational culture, occupational role performance, level of absorption in work, and subjective reactions to work. Like much of the previous literature, the current investigation analyzes work schedules in terms of the time demands they make on workers. It treats time as a fundamental resource for family life and examines the ways in which jobs impose demands on this scarce resource. The common denominator of time and its use becomes a way of linking work and family roles both theoretically and empirically.

On the other hand, this study provides more generous coverage of the dimensions of family life than of the dimensions of work. It includes consideration of three of these dimensions of family life. The most notable omission from this study concerns the dimension of family power — influence over family decisions.

Work Schedules

There has been a general background of interest and research on work schedules, starting perhaps in the 1950s with the study of shiftwork, a corollary of continuous-process production in the industrial economy. In the 1960s, new ideas about work schedules swept through industrial societies. "Flextime" was first proposed in Germany in 1965. The "compressed" four-day workweek was conceived shortly thereafter. More recently, both part-time work and "worksharing" (voluntary reductions in hours so as to reduce layoffs) have become topics of considerable interest. The term "alternative work schedules" (or "patterns") has arisen to encompass the whole range of these patterns of innovative schedules. The National Council on Alternative Work Patterns serves as the major clearinghouse for information on these issues. Perhaps the high point in the recent history of the alternative work-schedule movement was the passage of the Federal Employees Flexible and Compressed Work Schedules Act of 1978, which mandated implementation of flextime throughout the federal civil service.

Much of the available research on the relationship between work schedules and family life has concentrated on quite atypical work schedules, for example, flextime, shiftwork, and the four-day week. The present study departs from most previous research in that it attempts a systematic analysis of the major dimensions of the workweek. It adopts a dimensional, as opposed to a typological, approach and for the most part classifies work schedules according to four general dimensions applicable to all schedules. The first dimension, the pattern of days worked, focuses on whether the schedule calls for working the same days each week and whether it requires any weekend work. The second dimension, shift, is a familiar one and distinguishes among five shift categories: day, afternoon, night, rotating, and other irregular schedules. The number of hours worked each week, also a familiar notion, is the third dimension of work schedules. It should be pointed out that the first two dimensions, days and shift, concern how work-time is arranged or scheduled on a weekly and daily basis, respectively. By contrast, the third dimension, number of hours, addresses the issue of the amount of time worked.

Flexibility of schedule, the fourth dimension, concerns the degree to which workers have a choice in or control over the previous three dimensions of their work schedules. In the analysis to follow, flexibility is treated as a moderator variable, while the first three dimensions of work schedules function as predictors.

Taken together, the four dimensions do not capture all the possible differences among work schedules, but they do tap many of the important ones. In terms of the existing literature on schedules, the four pro- posed dimensions directly include the number of hours worked and shiftwork, and they treat the issue of flexibility raised by flextime as a more general dimension of schedules. But, admittedly, these four dimensions fail to capture the central issue raised by the four-day week, namely, the tradeoff between number of days worked in a week and number of hours worked in a day. It bears emphasizing that the major advantage of the dimensional approach to work schedules lies in its ability to classify all work schedules along a common set of meas- ures. For a national sample, in which the percentage of workers on special innovative schedules is extremely low, the generality of the dimensional approach has considerable appeal.

Measurement of work schedules differs somewhat in the case of two- earner families. The main variant is the inclusion of measures of the spouse's schedule that parallel the measures of the respondent's own schedule. In addition, the list of measures of schedule characteristics in the dual-earner case exceeds that used in the general analysis, and the scoring of some of the measures undergoes minor modifications for the special sample.

Family Life

In line with previous literature, the present study considers three major dimensions of the quality of family life: (1) amount of time spent each week in various family roles, including child care and housework, (2) degree of interference between work and family roles, and (3) level of family adjustment. Not included in the present study are certain dimensions of family life, marital decision-making power for example, that, although related to some occupational characteristics, have less relevance to variations in work schedules.

We extend the dimensional approach to work schedules into the measurement of family life. Few dimensions of family life are as basic as the allocation of time. In this study, we measure time spent in two family roles, child care and housework. Excluded, therefore, are meas- ures of time spent with one's spouse or time in other family roles. The study required respondents to estimate how much time they typically spend in various family activities on a daily basis. This method lacks the greater precision of time diaries (or time budgets) in which respon- dents keep a written record of how all time on a given day is spent (cf. Pleck, in press). Each method, of course, has its advantages and dis- advantages. The procedure based on time estimates is much simpler to administer; it provides data on a typical day (and, by inference, a typ- ical week) at the level of individuals. While the strategy using time diaries offers greater precision and avoids the systematically inflated time figures from the estimation procedure, it provides data on a typical day (or week) only at the aggregate level (that is, across individuals) because it samples only one or two *particular* days at the individual level.

The current investigation also measures time allocations in absolute rather than relative terms (cf. Pleck, in press). Certain other studies have inquired about the relative contributions of husband and wife to family roles such as child care (for example, husband's contribution equals 75 percent and wife's equals 25 percent, or husband's and wife's contributions both equal 50 percent). This proportional approach ignores differences in absolute amounts that may underlie the relative contributions of each spouse. It would seem better to measure temporal contributions separately and in absolute terms, and then generate relative scores as a subsequent measure, if necessary.

Hypotheses

The four central hypotheses tested for the sample of individual workers in this study concern the anticipated negative relationship between nonstandard work schedules and the quality of family life. These are that:

1. working a nonstandard pattern of days each week (weekend work, variable days) would be negatively related to the quality of the worker's family life;
2. working a nonstandard pattern of hours each day (afternoon, night, or rotating shift; variable hours) would be negatively related to the quality of the worker's family life;
3. working a large number of hours each week would be negatively related to the quality of the worker's family life; and
4. the negative effects of each of the foregoing nonstandard work schedules would be greater for workers with less flexibility in their schedules.

In addition to these four central hypotheses are certain less formal expectations about likely empirical relationships. Parallel to the fourth hypothesis, for example, is the general expectation that the negative effects of nonstandard schedules on family life will vary for demographic subgroups defined in terms of sex, presence of spouse, employment status of spouse, family life-cycle stage, and education. In Chapter 6, we discuss the possible relationships involving work schedules and family life among two-earner couples.

Research Design

The analyses described in this report follow an essentially standard regression strategy for relating independent variables (work schedule characteristics) to dependent variables (family life). As noted, in a departure from most previous research some of the analyses of dual-earner families include measures of the spouse's work schedule in addition to measures of the respondent's own work schedule as predictors of the respondent's family life.

Also somewhat distinctive is our method of handling moderator effects. Schedule flexibility has apparently never before been used as a moderator variable. Moreover, the moderated regression strategy used here for detecting interactions adopts a distinctly conservative approach to Type I errors. Imperfections remain, however, in this overall strategy for detecting interactions; included among them is the low power (and hence increased Type II error rate) of the statistical tests of interaction.

No special issues of research design arise in studying the relationship between a person's work schedule and his or her family life. The present study, however, also investigates the more complicated possibility that an individual's work schedule may affect the family life of other members of his or her family as well as influencing his or her own family life. The analysis of such cross-over effects requires attention to certain special issues of research design.

The present study allows the investigation of cross-over effects in the case of two-earner families. Two categories of cross-over effects are possible here: effects of the husband's schedule on his wife's family life and effects of the wife's schedule on her husband's family life. Our analysis procedure permits a statistical control on the respondent's work schedule when evaluating the effect of the spouse's work schedule on the respondent's family life.

The data analyzed in this study come from a nationally representative sample of American workers interviewed in the 1977 Quality of Employment Survey. To be sure, unusual, innovative, or otherwise interesting work schedules, including the special types discussed extensively in the literature, appear with low frequency in a national sample. Yet national samples do have substantial advantages. Within the limits of sampling error, *all* subgroups of workers in the national labor force appear in the sample in accordance with their representation in the population. As noted, although studies of work schedules and family life frequently omit employed women, this study includes an appropriate proportion of working women in the sample, thus giving proper emphasis to dual-earner families and to families headed by women. In the case of two-earner families, because each husband or wife interviewed was asked about his or her spouse's schedule, a sample of couples is effectively available for analyses of work schedules. This study is also sensitive to certain technical issues of sampling, including design effects and the underrepresentation of employed women (and certain other subgroups) that is associated with conventional procedures of respondent selection.

Review of the Previous Literature

Overview

Table 2.1 presents a summary of the relationships between different types of work schedules and different dimensions of family life based on findings from the studies reviewed. Most cells in the table have no entries, reflecting the constraints on current knowledge. What is known about work schedules and family life may be stated quite briefly. Long hours and shiftwork are associated with reductions in the quality of family life; flextime has positive relationships with some measures of family life; and the implications of work schedules for the spouse's family life have not been extensively demonstrated but appear stronger for working men than for working women.

Work Life. No assessment of recent trends in American work life can ignore certain major shifts in the composition of the labor force. Over the past twenty-five years, according to A. R. Miller's (1978) review of changing work patterns, there have been substantial changes in the proportion of the population engaged in market work and in the demographic composition of the work force. The nonworker-worker ratio has fluctuated widely, primarily as a reflection of the dramatic fluctuations in birth rates. Since 1965, for example, the ratio of nonworkers to workers has fallen precipitously, as would be expected given the declining birth rate. In addition, the long-term trends of increasing participation by women and declining years of work by men have accelerated. Specifically, young women appear to have been returning to the labor market much more quickly after the birth of their children, with a consequent reduction in their time out of the work force, and the customary retirement age of men has been falling. As a result, worklife patterns are becoming increasingly similar for men and women. Kanter (1978) observed that the labor force has also been getting younger and offered three reasons why: the youth bulge in the late 1960s and early 1970s (created by the post–World War II baby-

TABLE 2.1
Relationship between Work Schedules and
Family Life in Reviewed Studies

Work Schedule	Worker's Sex	Time Effect on		Conflict Effect on		Adjustment Effect on	
		Worker	Spouse	Worker	Spouse	Worker	Spouse
Number of	M	Negative	Positive	Positive	Positive	n.s.[a]	n.s.
Hours	F	Negative	n.s.	Positive	n.s.	—	—
Flextime	M & F	Positive	—[b]	Negative	—	—	—
Shiftwork	M	—	—	Positive	—	Negative	—
	F	—	—	Positive	—	—	—
Four-Day	M	Positive	—	—	—	n.s.	—
Week	F	—	—	—	—	—	—

[a]not significant.
[b]no data available.

boom generation), the decline in labor force participation of older people of both sexes, and the large increase in teenage labor force participation. Young (1980) has emphasized that the present labor force has a much higher ratio of college-educated persons than ever before.

A number of researchers have projected the demographic characteristics of the future labor force. According to Fullerton (1980), by the mid-1980s the number of persons in the labor force should exceed those not in the labor force, including babies. Present trends towards an increasingly female and college-educated labor force are expected to continue and minorities will become a larger proportion of the labor force. Yet, the recent trend toward a younger labor force will actually reverse as the baby-boom generation moves into the prime working age category (Freeman, 1979; Fullerton, 1980).

Compositional shifts along demographic lines do not constitute the only changes taking place in the occupational arena. Recent research has documented a number of trends in the work experiences reported by American workers. Staines and Quinn (1979), for example, have summarized changes over an eight-year period based on national surveys of workers in 1969, 1973, and 1977. They documented significant increases during the 1970s in workers' reports of availability of fringe benefits, underutilization of skills on the job, and the experience of being locked in to one's present job (that is, being unable to find alternative employment). On the other hand, significant decreases emerged in job satisfaction and in other measures of positive affect toward the job. Relatively unchanged over the eight-year period were the percentages of workers reporting a job-related illness or injury during the previous three years, age discrimination, race discrimination, irregular or unsteady employment, difficulties with transportation to and from work, and unpleasant physical working conditions.

Growing interest in the job-related experiences and problems of workers has extended beyond the monitoring of ongoing occupational trends and has generated a loose confederation of researchers, government officials, managers, trade unionists, and others who are committed to improving the quality of working life via efforts at planned change (Kerr and Rosow, 1979; Walton, 1980). Numerous innovations to enhance the quality of employment have been advanced and tried experimentally, and some have been widely adopted. Innovative work schedules such as flextime and the four-day week have drawn considerable interest as possible constructive modifications of the work environment.

Family Life. Demographic considerations are, likewise, of the utmost importance in understanding family life in this country. Weitzman (1978), for example, commented that the combination of sharp increases in the numbers and proportions of female heads of families and wives in the paid labor force represents one of the most striking modifications in the composition of American families. In recent years, statistics on the family have recorded a steady increase in the divorce rate, a decline in both the marriage and birth rates, and a rise in the ratio of out-of-wedlock births to total births. These trends translate into family structures in which an increasing proportion of children are members of single-parent families headed primarily by women (Kitagawa, 1981). Rates of both labor force participation and unemployment are higher among single mothers than among mothers in two-parent families. Women who head households with children also experience low levels of family income, frequently below the poverty line, and many require public assistance to meet the daily needs of family members (Waldman et al., 1979).

Our study gives special emphasis to families in which both husband and wife work for pay. The prevalence of such families has increased throughout this century, gradually replacing families in which only the husband is employed. According to Hayghe (1981), by 1968 the number and proportion of dual-earner families about equaled those of traditional-earner families (45 percent in each case). Over the ensuing decade, the number of dual-earner families rose by approximately one quarter, so that in 1978 51 percent of all married couples were dual-earner families while just 33 percent were of the traditional-earner type. In terms of several important demographic characteristics, two-worker families stand apart from their traditional counterparts. Members of dual-earner couples tend to be younger, better educated, and less likely to have preschool children; and, due to their combined salaries, they enjoy a substantially higher family income.

Interrelationship between Work Life and Family Life. Trends in family composition notwithstanding, much of the now considerable literature on the relationship between work life and family life sub-scribes implicitly to the traditional model of the family in which the husband is the breadwinner and the wife assumes responsibility for child rearing and homemaking. Since traditional concepts consider employment to be the norm for husbands and nonemployment the norm for wives, the perspective on social problems differs for the two sexes. Kanter (1977, p. 61) captured the point nicely:

> The sexual asymmetry is very apparent. It is the *unemployed man* who was seen as a social problem, likely to have disturbed marital relations and likely to produce delinquent children. For women, it was the *employed woman* who was seen in *virtually the same ways.* (italics in original)

Curiously, recent psychological studies of the effects of male unemployment on family life have been rare (but see Cobb and Kasl, 1977) despite the spate of studies conducted a generation ago in the context of the Depression (e.g., Angell, 1936; Bakke, 1940; Cavan, 1959). Instead, current literature on the effect of work on family life among males has raised a different issue, namely: What are the consequences for family life of the different kinds of jobs held by husbands? By comparison, the issue for females has for the most part remained: What are the consequences for family life of the wife's employment status (that is, working versus not working)? In short, in the case of husbands, efforts are made to differentiate among types of work environments; for wives, only the issue of employment typically commands attention.

Recent reviews of the literature on work and family life (e.g., Aldous et al., 1979; Kanter, 1977; Pleck, in press; Staines, 1980) have identified several major issues guiding empirical analyses of the effects on families of various dimensions of male employment:

1. the effects of the husband's occupational culture on the socialization of children: Do families socialize their children to have the personality characteristics, including values, that are necessary to adapt successfully to the occupational milieu in which the family breadwinner works? (See, for example, Aberle and Naegele, 1952; Kohn, 1969; Miller and Swanson, 1958);

2. the effects of the husband's occupational role performance on the

husband-wife exchange: Do husbands "exchange" their successful performance of the breadwinner role for their wives' fulfillment of traditional responsibilities in the family, thereby enhancing marital cohesion and solidarity? (See, for example, Dizard, 1968; Scanzoni, 1970);

3. the effects of the husband's level of absorption in work on family members: Do occupations that absorb and subsume much of workers' lives implicate other family members and command their direct participation in the work system in either its formal or informal aspects? (See, for example, Kanter, 1977; Papanek, 1975);

4. the effects of the husband's subjective reactions to work on his subjective reactions to family life: Is there a carry-over from positive attitudes toward work to positive assessments of marital and family life, and is there likewise a carry-over for negative work attitudes? (See, for example, Kemper and Reichler, 1976; Kornhauser, 1965; Staines, 1980); and

5. the effects of the husband's work schedule on family life (this topic is treated in detail below).

Other reviews of the literature on work and family life (e.g., Hoffman and Nye, 1974; Smith, 1979) have spelled out a corresponding set of issues for wives, each of which focuses on a different implication of the wife's employment status:

1. the effects of the wife's employment on children: Does maternal employment adversely affect children's development? (See, for example, Hoffman and Nye, 1974; Hoffman, 1979; Moore and Hofferth, 1979);

2. the effects of the wife's employment on marital adjustment: Does a wife's employment detract from her marital adjustment or from her husband's? (See, for example, Hofferth and Moore, 1979; Staines et al., 1978);

3. the effects of the wife's employment on marital power: Does working enhance a wife's marital power as reflected in her influence over family decision making? (See, for example, Blood and Hamblin, 1958; Heer, 1958);

4. the effects of the wife's employment on the marital division of labor: Do husbands engage in more child care and housework when their wives are employed? (See, for example, Blood and Wolfe, 1960; Robinson, 1977); and

5. the effects of the wife's employment on her overall psychological adjustment and well-being: Do working wives score differently from housewives on various measures of physical and mental health? (See, for example, Feld, 1963; Ferree, 1976).

Work Schedules and Family Life. Although our study concerns itself primarily with the effects of work schedules on family life, a number of the issues cited earlier also pertain to the patterns of working hours. The number of hours worked per week, for example, is one measure of a husband's performance in the exchange between husbands and wives. The amount of time invested in the work role is, likewise, an indicator of a husband's level of absorption in his work.

For all the recent interest in the relationship between work life and family life, surprisingly little is known about the impact of work schedules on families. Yet the amount of time demanded by occupations and the timing of occupational events are, as Kanter (1977, p. 31) observed, among the most obvious and important ways that occupational life affects family life:

> Family events and routines are built around work rhythms (at least more generally than the reverse), just as much of the timing of events in the society as a whole (e.g., the opening and closing of stores, which television programs are shown at night) is predicated on assumptions about the hours, days, and months when people are most likely to be working or not working. The sheer number of hours spent at work as well as which part of the day those hours encompass can influence a large number of family processes through, for example, the effects of fatigue or the availability of the worker to take responsibility for or participate in family events. Whether work-related activities extend beyond the formal hours officially devoted to "work" and intrude upon time the family expects to claim can similarly affect the quality of family life. How the hours which workers have available for leisure and family synchronize with those of the other family members and the possibilities which society makes available for those hours is another issue. Finally, work which does not permit stable daily rhythms to develop or disrupts daily routines — such as work which involves a great deal of travel — also constrains the possibilities for family organization.

The available empirical literature on the impact of work schedules on families leaves much to be desired. There are no studies that measure the major dimensions of work schedules and family life and then systematically relate these measures. Instead, small numbers of studies have concentrated on unusual schedules — whether innovations primarily in the pattern of days worked, as in the case of the four-day week, or atypical patterns of hours, as in the case of flextime and shiftwork. In addition, one limited and rather fragmented set of studies has examined the effects of the total number of hours worked per week on family life.

But perhaps the most glaring fault in the empirical literature on working hours and family life is the serious underrepresentation of working women, especially in the context of shiftwork and the four-day week. This is particularly ironic since stronger associations between work schedules and family life might be expected among women than among men. For the most part, women are mentioned in reported studies only as wives of male workers, and only infrequently is it suggested that some of them might be working wives. One important implication of this scholarly neglect of working women is, of course, the lack of attention given to families in which the husband and wife both work and to the special problems in scheduling work and family activities that such families have to face (e.g., Keith and Schafer, 1980; Rapoport and Rapoport, 1971). In fairness, it should be pointed out that the more recent literature on work schedules and family life has shown an increased awareness of the issues involving female employment and two-earner families.

Number of Hours Worked Per Week

A number of different approaches are available for examining workers' degree of temporal involvement in their work. Several special types of work schedules, for example, raise the issue of the amount of time spent at work: part-time employment, work sharing (or short-time), overtime, and multiple job holding (or moonlighting). The approach selected here is to focus simply on the number of hours a worker works each week, thereby adopting a common currency in which the foregoing special schedules as well as all other work schedules may conveniently be compared.

Current evidence on the total amount of time worked per week indicates a generally decelerating reduction over the last century. Hedges and Taylor (1980, p. 4) have summarized the relevant history:

> From 1900 to 1946, the average workweek shrank from about 53 to 44 hours. Productivity growth and declining agricultural employment underlay this trend, which was rapid in some periods and arrested, or even reversed, in others. For example, the average workweek declined substantially during the Great Depression, as work-sharing efforts led to Federal legislation which set the standard workweek and workday (beyond which premium pay was required) below the pre-Depression level. During World War II, average weekly hours lengthened, but government controls on wages coupled with competition for workers resulted in substantial gains in paid vacations.
>
> Since the 1940's, worktime has been further reduced by the growth of service industries and the continued decline of agriculture and the increased employment of women and youth. Rising expectations and inflation probably have exerted counter pressures. On balance, hours reductions have proceeded slowly. Some analysts, considering only the hours of

men have concluded that little or no change in weekly hours has occurred in the United States in the post–World War II era.

The same authors have also summarized more recent trends, adding an international comparison (pp. 4–5):

> The average workweek for nonagricultural wage and salary employees who usually work full time declined from 43.0 to 42.6 hours, or nearly half an hour between May 1968 and May 1979. The decline reflected a decrease of almost 3 percentage points in the proportion of persons at work 41 to 48 hours, with a commensurate increase in the proportion at work from 35 to 39 hours.
>
> The increased prevalence of women and youth in the work force and the growth of industries with shorter than average workweeks contributed to the reduction in weekly hours. Other factors included changes in the Fair Labor Standards Act (FLSA) and in collective bargaining agreements and an increase in unemployment....
>
> Although economic systems and labor force statistics vary by country, available information on workweeks in Canada and Western Europe also shows hours reductions in the past decade. For example, manufacturing workers in Canada averaged 38.9 hours of work per week in May 1979, down from 40.6 hours in May 1968.

It bears emphasis that decreases in the average workweek have derived from several sources: changes in the demographic and occupational composition of the labor force, including the expansion of part-time work (Owen, 1979); increased use of paid holidays and paid vacations; and, of course, actual reductions in the workweek (Bohen and Viveros-Long, 1981). Two other potential sources of change, overtime work and moonlighting, appear not to have had much effect on the average workweek over the last decade (Hedges and Taylor, 1980).

Time Spent in Family Roles. The amount of time spent at work should presumably be negatively related to the time spent in family roles. To a substantial degree, it is. One of the earliest relevant studies adopted the occupation as the unit of analysis. Gerstl's (1961) comparison of professors, dentists, and advertising executives established that the average worktimes for these three occupational groups of men were inversely related to somewhat crude measures of the amount of time each group spent with their children and on household chores (no significance tests cited).

By contrast, subsequent (and more sophisticated) studies have all taken the individual worker as the unit of analysis. The data on the relationship between paid work and housework have proven generally consistent. A Canadian study of married couples (Meissner et al., 1975) reported a negative relationship among wives between hours in paid employment and hours spent on housework (no significance tests). Walker and Woods (1976) obtained negative relationships among both husbands and wives between hours employed and hours devoted to household tasks (no significance tests). Robinson (1977) likewise detected negative relationships for both sexes between work time and time on housework (cooking, laundry, marketing, etc.). The empirical pattern for other domestic roles examined in Robinson's study is less clear. Among husbands, the number of hours worked was negatively associated with time spent on general household obligations (e.g., gardening, shopping, errands) but unrelated to time spent with children. Among wives, nonlinear relationships emerged between work time and time spent on general household obligations and on child care (no significance tests).

Several other investigations of the relationships between time allocated to work and to family roles have departed from the relevant research paradigm and, perhaps in consequence, have obtained fewer significant, consistent, and interpretable results. This is true of recent studies by Clark and his colleagues (Clark and Gecas, 1977; Clark et al., 1978) and also of studies by Stafford et al. (1977) and Perrucci et al. (1978). All four studies involved either measures or samples that fall short of ideal for investigating relationships among time allocations.

The negative association between work time and time spent on housework and related household chores, while empirically established, should not be overstated. One less hour of work time does not mean one more hour of domestic work. Among men, for example, Robinson's (1977) data indicate that an increase (or decrease) of one hour of paid work was associated with a change of only about one-fifth of an hour of housework and household chores; in the case of women, the change was only about one-tenth of an hour.[1] In econometric language, time spent on housework and related chores is relatively inelastic with respect to changes in paid work, especially for wives.

Interference between Work and Family Life. The amount of work time should generate a positive relationship with the experience of interference (or conflict) between work and family life. Empirical evidence in this case fully confirms expectation. In a study of two-earner families, Keith and Schafer (1980) found that the total hours spent working each week (on the main job plus additional jobs) was the strongest significant predictor of work/family strain for both sexes. Mortimer (1980) developed an overall index of temporal requirements imposed by work, which included measures of time spent on the main job plus second jobs, as well as a question about working under the pressure of time. This index of temporal requirements was positively and significantly associated with work/family strain for her sample of married, male, college graduates, most of whom were in the early phases of professional or managerial careers.

Family Adjustment. Time spent at work might also be thought to affect family adjustment and perhaps other qualitative aspects of family life as well, yet fewer relationships have emerged than expected. Ridley (1973) studied the relationship between the amount of time devoted to the occupational role in excess of the normal workday (a six-item scale tapping time devoted to reading, writing, talking, thinking about the job) and marital adjustment (a nine-item scale) among a sample of married, female school teachers and their husbands. Ridley obtained no significant association between the two concepts among either the teachers or their husbands. Mortimer (1980) detected no zero-order association between the temporal dimension of the husband's job and his marital satisfaction; however, a path-analytic model that used mediating family variables to separate direct and indirect effects did establish a significant connection between temporal requirements and marital satisfaction. Piotrkowski and Crits-Christoph (1981) studied the relationship between (multiple) characteristics of women's jobs and their family adjustment in a sample of ninety-nine women in dual-earner families. The investigators divided the ninety-nine wives into two groups, those with occupations of high prestige and those in less prestigious occupations, and conducted separate analyses for the two groups. Based on multiple regressions with six job-related predictors, Piotrkowski and Crits-Christoph found that for neither group did time spent at work (one of the six predictors) bear any relationship to even one of the three indices of marital adjustment.

Taking a different approach, Clark et al. (1978) noted that husbands' self-reported work time had no effect on their competence in housekeeper, social supporter, sexual, and recreational roles, as judged by their wives. Clark and Gecas (1977) found that fathers' self-reported work time had no effect on their competence in two parental roles, child care and child socialization, again as rated by their wives.

Impact on the Spouse's Family Life. Several studies have asked whether the amount of time people work is related to their spouses' family life. The answer to this question about cross-over effects appears to be affirmative only for working men and not for working women. Walker and Woods (1976), for example, found that as husbands' work time increases, the amount of time their wives spend on housework also increases (no signficance tests). Nonetheless, two studies failed to find a relationship between the wives' hours of employment and their husbands' hours of housework (Meissner et al., 1975; Walker and Woods, 1976).

The data based on work/family conflict as the measure of quality of family life display a similar asymmetry by sex. That is, the husband's work time relates positively to his wife's work/family interference, but her work time bears no relationship to his level of interference. Greenhaus and Kopelman (1981) reported relevant data from a sample of male graduates from an eastern technical college. The investigators noted that for two-earner families, the wives' time involvement at work (part-time versus full-time) had no effect on the presence or intensity of their husbands' work/family conflict. Keith and Schafer (1980) analyzed data on work/family role strain based on a sample of 135 two-earner families. The predictors in their multiple regressions included the respondent's total number of hours worked per week and the spouse's total number of hours worked, along with selected demographic and other variables. For both sexes, the number of hours one spouse worked was a positive predictor of that person's own work/family role strain, and, interestingly, an increase in the husband's number of work hours was associated with an elevation in the wife's level of strain—but not vice versa.

Marital adjustment provides yet another perspective on the spouse's family life. Clark et al. (1978) found that husbands' work time did not show any significant effect on their wives' marital satisfaction when husbands' income and education, wives' education and work time, and the presence of preschoolers or school-age children in the home were controlled.

Summary. For both sexes, large amounts of time spent at work are associated with less time in certain family roles (mainly housework and general household chores) and elevated levels of work/family interference. Restricted to samples of men, existing studies of the relationship between number of hours worked and various dimensions of family adjustment have failed to uncover any direct associations. Studies of the cross-over effect suggest a possible sexual asymmetry: A husband's work time may be associated with an increase in his wife's level of work/family conflict, but *her* temporal involvement in work appears unrelated to *his* experience of conflict.

Flextime

Flextime actually covers a variety of schedule arrangements in which workers exercise some control over the hours they work. Typically, a core period of time in the middle of the day is mandatory for all workers, but certain variations in starting (and hence finishing) times are permitted. When management requires workers to maintain the same schedule each day, at least for some extended period of time, the arrangement is called "fixed flextime" or "staggered hours"; the term "gliding time" enters when workers decide anew each day what their pattern of hours will be (Swart, 1978). Flextime, in short, introduces the notion of flexibility of work schedules in conjunction with the notion of workers' choice or control.

Most scholars agree that flextime has become more common in the U.S. over the last half-decade. Its actual prevalence, however, has proven more difficult to estimate reliably than has been true of other nontraditional work schedules. Nollen and Martin (1978) estimated that the total U.S. labor force contained 2.5 to 3.5 million workers on flextime, excluding self-employed workers and those professionals, managers, and sales people who have always set their own hours. Hedges and Mellor (1981) estimated that, in May 1980, 7.6 million workers were on flextime, or 12 percent of all those in full-time, non-farm, wage-and-salary jobs. By comparison, Western European countries have embraced flextime more enthusiastically. Rates of adoption are high, for example, in West Germany, France, and Switzerland, reaching as high as 40 percent in parts of German-speaking Switzerland (Owen, 1979; Swart, 1978).

Although the advocates of flextime as a solution to many family problems are legion, present evidence justifies only a modest level of optimism. Winett and Neale (1980a) reviewed forty-three studies of flextime but found just eight that inquired into family practices affected by flextime. These inquiries generally amounted to only a few items on questionnaires administered after but not before the introduction of flextime. According to Winett and Neale, although the responses recorded in the eight studies are suggestive of more available family time and greater ease in child care arrangements, the questions' superficiality cannot be disputed. A more recent investigation (Rainey and Wolf, 1981) extended to nine this list of somewhat superficial survey reports on flextime and family life.

Time Spent in Family Roles. Winett et al. (1982; also Winett and Neale, 1980b) conducted quasi-experimental studies of the effects of fixed flextime on family life at two agencies of the federal government. Using a nonequivalent control group design at each agency, the investigators collected time budget and attitudinal data from workers who opted for a flextime program (which permitted them to change their daily schedule by about an hour) and also from those who remained on regular hours because of commuter arrangements, spouse's work hours, or personal preference. The quasi-experiments included workers in secretarial and administrative positions at each agency, all of whom had at least one child under age thirteen. Participants were drawn from both sexes. In general, the workers on flextime chose to arrive at and depart from work significantly earlier than before the change in schedule.

At the first agency, the switch from a baseline period of five weeks to a period of fourteen weeks of flextime was accompanied by significant increases in the amount of evening time workers spent with their spouses and with their children (amounting to a significant increment of over one hour in total family time). This pattern of increases over time was not duplicated among workers remaining on regular hours.

At the second agency, the researchers collected data before flextime and then for three periods during flextime: spring, summer, and fall. The phases allowed for examination of seasonal effects and corresponded to the school attendance of children. The overall time spent with family decreased by about twenty minutes in the morning but then increased by about thirty-seven minutes in the evening for those on fixed flexible hours, compared with an increase at night of only about five minutes for those on regular hours. No changes attributable to the alteration of work schedules were reported in weekend activities. Both schedule groups tended to increase family-related time during the summer; generally, differences between the groups dissipated somewhat by the fall. Moreover, time spent with family members varied by family composition; for example, sole breadwinning fathers spent less evening time with their children than did mothers in two-earner families.

Bohen and Viveros-Long (1981) compared reports of family life from personnel at two federal agencies, one on fixed flextime and one on standard hours. At each agency, the survey sample included slightly more men than women. Workers in the survey estimated how much time they typically spent on two family roles (child care and housework) during workdays and off days, thus making possible a computation of estimated average weekly hours spent on each role. The type of work schedule did not make a significant difference in the time workers allocated to child care. Yet, male and female workers on flextime spent significantly more time on housework (two and three hours more per week, respectively) than did workers on standard hours. Interestingly, a corresponding difference did not emerge for the total sample (with males and females pooled), presumably because of the large within-schedule-group variance created by the sizeable mean difference between the hours reported by the two sexes. Bohen and Viveros-Long also included measures of the division of domestic labor between husband and wife — percentage of total child care and, separately, total housework performed by the worker (versus his or her spouse). Their research thus raises the interesting possibility that flextime may increase the amount of time that wives spend in family roles and thereby render even more inequitable the traditional division of domestic labor between husbands and wives. For neither family role, however, did the division of labor differentiate between those on flextime and those working standard hours.

Interference between Work and Family Life. Winett et al. (1982; Winett and Neale, 1980b) reported analyses relevant to the subject of work/family interference. Their questionnaire included items concerning the difficulty of coordinating aspects of family life, particularly with respect to hours of work (for example, spending time with one's children). Although preflextime scores of the flextime and control groups did not differ significantly at either government agency, the introduction of flextime made a difference at both agencies. Workers on flexible hours found it significantly easier to coordinate work schedules with afternoon and evening time with their children, time with their spouse during the week, and time on shopping and chores.

Bohen and Viveros-Long (1981) compared data on personnel from the two government agencies in their study using two indices of work/family stress. For the total sample and for both the male and female subsamples, people on flextime reported significantly less stress on both indices than did those on standard time.

The degree of association between flextime and decrements in work/family stress varied by family composition, but not in the expected ways. According to Bohen and Viveros-Long (p. 129):

> For the stress measures in this study, the most telling finding is that the flexitime workers who have less stress than their standard time counterparts are individuals without primary responsibility for children, namely, married women without children, fathers whose wives are not employed, and single adults without children. The primary group whose family lives were expected to benefit from more flexible work schedules, namely, employed mothers, did not report less stress than those mothers on standard schedules.

A limited program of fixed flextime may benefit workers with modest family responsibilities and minor logistical problems; but for groups having far greater complexities in combining work and family life (e.g., employed mothers) a restricted program of fixed flextime does little to reduce work/family stress.

Unlike some of the other nontraditional work schedules, the effect of flextime on family adjustment or the cross-over effects of one person's flextime on his or her spouse's experience of family life have never received serious study.

Summary. Flextime appears to increase family time by small amounts. In one pair of quasi-experimental studies, workers on flextime went to work earlier in the day and sacrificed a limited amount of (less enjoyable) family time in the morning in return for a larger gain of (more enjoyable) family time in the evening. In another investigation, workers on flextime spent more time on housework than did other workers. In addition, flextime has been shown to be related to lower work/family conflict but not among those groups of workers who, because of major family responsibilities, suffer the greatest stress and are most in need of relief. Finally, the associations between flextime and two other factors—family adjustment and spouse's family life—lie outside the scope of available information.

Shiftwork

Without doubt, one pattern of working hours with dramatic impact on family life is shiftwork. Yet the concept of shiftwork proves highly complex. Shift systems may take many different forms, depending on whether there are three shifts or two, whether the shifts are worked during the day or at night, and whether the work is continuous (without a break at the weekend) or semicontinuous (with a break at the weekend). Within any particular shift system, an important additional distinction arises between fixed and rotating shifts. On the fixed shift schedule, the same hours of the day are worked each week; on the rotating schedule, the span of hours worked changes periodically.

The difference between fixed and rotating shifts may be illustrated in the context of the three-shift system. Compared to the conventional work pattern of a morning start followed by a span of eight or so working hours (day work), the fixed shift in the three-shift system involves a stable daily schedule but an unconventional starting time, either in the late afternoon (afternoon shift) or in the evening (night shift). Rotating shifts typically require successive periods of daywork, afternoon shifts, and night shifts in some specified order, with the period of each of the three shifts varying from as little as a few days to as much as several weeks. Within the general category of rotating shifts, still further differentiation is possible. One of the better-known subcategories of rotating shifts is the split shift, in which the worker has a break in working hours ranging from one to eight hours. The fixed and rotating patterns associated with three-shift and two-shift systems do not by any means exhaust all of the possible patterns of working hours. Many irregular and idiosyncratic work schedules exist, and sometimes it is difficult to know whether or not they can be viewed as belonging to subcategories of shiftwork.

Working in shifts, especially night work, has been known for a long time, but the steadily increasing industrialization during this century has made shiftwork a major fixture of modern western economies (Agervold, 1976; Maurice, 1975; Walker, 1978; Zalusky, 1978). Hedges and Sekscenski (1979, p. 15) summarize trends in the prevalence of shiftwork in the U.S. over the last two decades:

> Payroll data for manufacturing plants, available for 1960–61 forward, indicate that a 15-year upward trend in the proportion of plant workers on second and third shifts was arrested, at least temporarily, in the mid-1970's. After rising from 22.1 percent in 1960–61 to 28.9 percent in 1973–75, the proportion declined to 26.8 percent in 1976. More recent annual data from household surveys show no growth from 1973 to 1978 in the proportion of factory operatives on late shifts.

According to the same U.S. report, roughly one in six full-time, non-farm, wage-and-salary employees works on a shift other than the typical daytime schedule; and although men generally remain overrepresented, in some industries the proportion of women on nonday shifts equals or exceeds that of men.

Time Spent in Family Roles. No published studies offer hard evidence as to whether shiftwork is associated with any change in the actual amount of time workers spend in family roles and, if so, in which direction. Such evidence and speculation as do exist tend to be inconsistent across studies (e.g., Carpentier and Cazamian, 1977; Chadwick-Jones, 1969; Guerin and Durrmeyer, 1973; Maurice and Monteil, 1965; Mott et al., 1965; Walker, 1978).

Interference between Work and Family Life. The bulk of the evidence linking shiftwork to family life concerns whether shiftwork is associated with elevated levels of work/family interference. Not all studies, however, include appropriate statistical comparisons between shiftworkers and employees working days. Some investigations report only that a certain (and sometimes substantial) proportion of shiftworkers complain of work/family conflicts (e.g., Bast, 1960; Mann and Hoffman, 1960; Maurice and Monteil, 1965; Philips Factory, 1958; Ulich, 1957). Other studies merely record the judgments of shiftworkers that they experience more work/family strain than they have experienced or would experience on a regular daytime schedule (e.g., Drenth et al., 1976; Mott et al., 1965; Wyatt and Marriott, 1953). Still other investigations compare shiftworkers and daytime workers but do so in such small numbers as to preclude statistical generalization (e.g., Hood and Golden, 1979; Lein et al., 1974).

The study by Mott et al. (1965), unquestionably one of the most extensive investigations of shiftwork, illustrates how problems of research design and analysis strategy can limit the utility of empirical findings. Using a sample of white, male, blue-collar workers in continuous-process industries in the east-central part of the United States, the researchers collected data through questionnaires from day workers and shiftworkers and also from the wives of shiftworkers. The first problem with their study is that workers on nonday shifts (afternoon, night, rotating) were asked to compare their current shift with a steady day schedule in terms of difficulty in engaging in various marital and parental activities. Mott's data thus include no analytic comparisons between the work/family interference reported by shiftworkers and day workers, only the judgments of shiftworkers comparing interference under the two types of schedules (and finding it greater under conditions of shiftwork). Second, in their analytic comparisons of levels of work/family interference among the three nonday shifts, Mott et al. performed one-way analyses of variance and omnibus F tests but included no pairwise t tests. As a result, it is unclear which pairs of shifts are significantly different.

Several other studies, nonetheless, do include relevant comparisons between the levels of work/family interference reported by shift and day workers. Young and Willmott (1973) asked husbands in a London sample whether their work interfered with their family life. A majority of the shiftworkers (52 percent) replied affirmatively, compared to only a third of the weekend workers (34 percent) and a quarter of the other workers (27 percent) (chi-square significant). House (1980) studied the effects of shiftwork among a population of nonmanagerial factory workers. However, his index of job-nonjob conflict included three items, only one of which asked about work/family strain. Based on an analysis sample of white males, House reported a significantly positive relationship between shiftwork (generally the 3 p.m.–11 p.m. shift) and job-nonjob conflict, even after the imposition of multivariate controls.

A third study, and the only one to include female shiftworkers, offers the most extensive evidence linking shifts and work/family conflict. Tasto et al. (1978) analyzed data from two samples, food processors (71 percent male) and nurses (98 percent female). Shiftworkers reported significantly more interference than other workers between their work hours and their sexual activities. Among food processors, night shiftworkers reported the most interference, followed in order by rotators, afternoon shiftworkers, and workers on day shift. Exactly the same ordering emerged from the data on nurses. Tasto et al. also employed a more indirect measure of work/family conflict — satisfaction with the amount of time able to be spent with various family members. Each shift of food processors reported significantly less satisfaction with the amount of time spent with their spouses than did those working on day-time schedules. This was true of nurses, too. For both samples, rotators and night shiftworkers were more dissatisfied on this item than after-noon shiftworkers, who were in turn more dissatisfied than day shift-workers. Similarly, all other food-processor shift categories were signif-icantly more dissatisfied than were day shiftworkers with the amount of time they had available to spend with their children. Afternoon and rotating shift food processors were the least satisfied. In the case of nurses, rotators were clearly the most dissatisfied group.

The only evidence casting any doubt about the negative effects of shiftwork on family life comes from a study in which employees worked on the shift of their choice (de la Mare and Walker, 1968). Night workers registered lower scores than people on other shifts (day and rotating) on two measures of work/family interference (difficulty in organizing the household routine to fit their work schedules, oppor-tunities for family life) but no significant differences emerged on a third (opportunity for helping with domestic chores). De la Mare and Walker's study raises the interesting possibility that when work sched-ules are flexible and those who work on shifts do so by choice, the effects of shiftwork on work/family conflict may be diminished and shiftwork may even reduce such conflict.

Of additional interest are the findings of Mott et al. (1965) comparing work/family conflict for the three nonday shifts (with omnibus F tests but no pairwise t tests). According to the data on husbands, rotating shifts consistently create high levels of interference with various com-ponents of the marital role (e.g., assisting wives with housework, providing diversion and relaxation, sexual relations, and decision making). Afternoon and night shifts generate roughly equal but lower levels of interference with marital activities. Data on interference with the parental role present a different pattern. Among fathers on shift-work, the afternoon shift reportedly interferes much more than do the other two shifts with a variety of parental activities (e.g., companion-ship with children, teaching useful skills, control and discipline).[2]

Family Adjustment. Only the study by Mott et al. (1965) evaluated the connection between shiftwork and marital adjustment. In this part of the analysis, fortunately, the statistical comparisons involving hus-bands included the day shift along with the earlier three nonday shifts, although again the statistical testing included F tests but not t tests. According to the data on three indices of marital adjustment (marital happiness, avoidance of friction, coordination of family activities), adjustment among husbands is highest for those on the day shift. Differences among the three nonday shifts lack consistency across indices of adjustment, but Mott et al. did not test the significance of these differences.

Impact on the Spouse's Family Life.. Although several studies have investigated whether shiftwork affects the family life of the shift-worker's spouse (i.e., cross-over effects), problems of research design seriously complicate the interpretation of the data. These methodological problems overlap with those in the preceding investigations of the shiftworker's own family life. With few exceptions (e.g., Tasto et al., 1978), the studies of spouses' responses to shiftwork confine themselves to the traditional type of family — an employed husband (shiftworker) and a nonemployed wife (housewife). Moreover, a number of investigations have requested husbands to report on the feelings of their wives rather than allowing the wives to speak for themselves (e.g., Andersen, 1970; de la Mare and Walker, 1968; Mann and Hoffman, 1960; Tasto et al., 1978); some studies have reported the attitudes of wives to their husbands' shiftwork but did not inquire directly about its impact on family life (e.g., Mann and Hoffman, 1960); other researchers asked family members to compare two work schedules rather than measuring attitudes to each separately and then comparing the two statistically (e.g., Banks, 1956; Brown, 1959; Chadwick-Jones, 1969; Drenth et al., 1976); and still other research encountered the problem of too few cases for quantitative analysis (Hood and Golden, 1979; Lein et al. 1974). In addition, virtually all previous studies have failed to control for the husband's reports on his family life when examining the relationship between his shiftwork and his wife's assessment of her family life.

The only study that survives the most serious of these methodological objections is Mott et al. (1965), a comparison of the work/family interference reported by the wives of men on nonday shifts. The investigators observed that shift interference with the marital role was notably low among wives of men on afternoon shifts (as opposed to night or rotating), whereas it was notably high among husbands on rotating shifts (no pairwise t tests). Moreover, the husbands' shift schedules were unrelated to the ease or difficulty with which wives performed the parental role even though the afternoon shift was accompanied by special problems for the parental role among husbands. In addition, Mott et al. found that comparisons among the wives of the three groups of shiftworkers yielded no significant differences on any of the three indices of marital adjustment.

Summary. Few people have attempted to justify the adoption of shiftwork on the basis of its positive effects on workers and certainly not in terms of its impact on their family life. Although current re-search has not yet established whether shiftwork affects the amount of time that workers spend with their families, it does indicate that shift-work is associated with increased levels of interference between work and family life. The relationship between shiftwork and interference may weaken, however, when workers can select their shifts. Compari-sons among the three nonday shifts suggest that rotating shifts are asso-ciated with substantial conflict between work and all family roles and, further, that night shifts are associated with more problems for the marital role than are afternoon shifts, although this ordering is reversed for the paternal role. Shiftwork also relates negatively to workers' marital adjustment. Efforts to consider spouses' responses to shiftwork have foundered on methodological problems. As a general rule, exist-ing studies of shiftwork leave a great deal of room for improvement in both research design and statistical analysis.

The Four-Day Week

The four-day, forty-hour (or 4/40) workweek, also known as the compressed workweek, represents one of the more recent departures from the traditional five-day, forty-hour (or 5/40) workweek. Hedges (1980) reported a trend from 1973 to 1979 toward fewer but longer workdays for full-time, nonfarm workers. She noted that the compres-sion of weekly hours into fewer days was evident both below and above the forty-hour standard workweek but, interestingly, the special case of the 4/40 workweek has not been adopted widely. After a small in-crease between 1973 and 1977 (from 1.0 to 1.4 percent), it no more than kept pace with the overall growth in wage-and-salary employ-ment between 1977 and 1979.

Few investigations have directly explored the effects of the four-day workweek on family life. Some surveys have asked workers not on the compressed week whether or not they would chose the 4/40 schedule and the reasons for their decision. Such surveys give workers a chance to mention factors involving their family life (e.g., Dickinson and Wijting, 1975; Kenny, 1974). Four other surveys requested workers who were currently on a compressed week to assess the effects of the switch to the 4/40. Hodge and Tellier (1975) reported that some workers mentioned that the compacted schedule permitted them more time with family members and on housework. Steele and Poor (1970) asked workers to list the leisure activities they engaged in regularly on their four-day schedule and also those they had previously participated in when on a five-day schedule. Spending time with family was reportedly more often a regular activity when on the four-day schedule. Nord and Costigan (1973) collected three waves of data from employees of a pharmaceutical company that had switched from a 5/40 to a 4/38 schedule. Workers' initial evaluations of the effects of the change on family life were predominantly favorable, but a year later unfavorable reactions edged out favorable ones. Also at the one-year mark, men were significantly less likely than women to indicate favorable changes in home life; and people with one or more children living at home felt significantly less positive than those with no children at home. The fourth survey report was more anecdotal than quantitative (Swerdloff, 1975).

Time Spent in Family Roles. By far the most intensive study of the effects of the four-day week on family life is Maklan's (1977a; 1977b) investigation of a sample of male, blue-collar workers in Michigan and Minnesota. The study compared the responses of workers on four-day workweeks with those of workers on five-day schedules. The research design included structured, personal interviews of respondents and time-budget diaries in which respondents recorded their activities for one workday and for the preceding or following nonworkdays. The diary provided information concerning the activities engaged in, their duration, and whether they involved other members of the family. In reporting on Maklan's data, we focus on time allocations to two family roles—child care and housework; here and subsequently, we exclude any forms of child care from the list of activities counted as housework. Maklan noted that four-day workers spent a great deal more time with their children when compared to five-day workers (no significance tests).[3] In the case of housework, he observed minimal differences between the four- and five-day workers regarding hours spent on traditionally female housework (grocery shopping, cooking, washing dishes, and laundry). As for more traditionally male household chores (home repairs, maintenance of heat and water systems, and shopping for goods and services other than groceries), four-day workers contributed substantially more time.

Family Adjustment. Maklan hypothesized that, owing to their greater flexibility in organizing family-related activities, four-day workers would express greater satisfaction with their conjugal and parental role performances and with their marriages in general than would a comparable group of five-day workers. Maklan found, however, virtually no differences between the two groups in mean satisfaction scores on the three dependent variables. Yet this did not mean that the four-day work schedule proved unrelated to adjustment in the family setting. Whereas, on average, four-day and five-day men expressed equal satisfaction, there were marked differences in the distributions of their responses on the measures of satisfaction with conjugal role performance and with marriage. Five-day workers indicated feeling moderately satisfied with conjugal role performance and marriage. Four-day workers, on the other hand, gave significantly more extreme responses.

Summary. The effects of the compressed workweek on family life have not been extensively studied. According to the best available investigation (Maklan, 1977a; 1977b), the 4/40 schedule is positively related to the amount of time husbands devote to child care and to traditionally male home chores, but compacted schedules do not differ from standard schedules in terms of mean levels of family adjustment. Unfortunately, Maklan's analysis included no explicit measures of work/family interference. In general, it bears emphasis that the current literature tells us little about the effects of the 4/40 schedule on the family life of working women and, likewise, little about its effects on the family life of spouses regardless of their sex. Also, the four-day week raises questions about how time on weekends, including long weekends, is distributed among work, family, and leisure. One of the few other contexts in which this important issue is considered is rotating shiftwork. In neither case does existing research spell out clearly the implications for families of different ways of spending weekends.

Notes

1. These tradeoffs from Robinson's data should not be confused with his report (pp. 54–55) on tradeoffs between work and nonfreetime activities (i.e., one hour of work corresponds to .35 hours of nonfreetime among employed men and to .43 hours among employed women) because his category of nonfreetime includes child care and personal care as well as housework and related chores.

2. Mott et al. also repeated their analytic comparisons of the three nonday shifts for two subgroups: workers wanting to change their shifts and those desiring no change.

3. Maklan (1977b) explained that some, but by no means all, of this difference was attributable to one four-day worker who rushed his daughter to the hospital and subsequently spent a great deal of time with her.

3

Survey Methodology: Sample, Analysis Strategy, and Measures[1]

Sample

The Quality of Employment Surveys

The data for this study come from the 1977 Quality of Employment Survey, the latest in a series of three national surveys of American workers conducted by the University of Michigan's Institute for Social Research. The survey series was designed to provide reliable national data on the working conditions of employed adults and on the behaviors, problems, and attitudes associated with employment.

The first of these surveys, the 1969–70 Survey of Working Conditions, was conducted with a representative sample of employed American adults during November and December, 1969. The essential descriptive data of that survey, together with methodological details and some limited interpretive comments were published in 1971 (Quinn and Associates). The second survey, the 1972–73 Quality of Employment Survey,[2] obtained data from a sample of workers comparable to that of the 1969 survey. This second data collection took place from January to March 1973. A statistical reference volume was issued for this study also (Quinn and Shepard, 1974).

A third national survey was initiated in 1977, with data collected from October to December of that year — almost five years after the 1973 data collection. It was sponsored by several agencies of the U.S. Department of Labor and coordinated by the Office of the Assistant Secretary for Policy, Evaluation and Research. The sponsoring agencies were the Employment and Training Administration, the Employment

Standards Administration, the Occupational Safety and Health Administration, and the Labor Management Services Administration.

The central aims of the 1977 survey were in line with those of the two previous surveys: to obtain a third measurement of certain basic or "core" variables for use in trend assessment and to extend the survey content to include selected new and enlarged topics. However, a major change in the survey design was introduced: provisions were made to interview not only a representative cross-section sample of employed adult workers, but also to reinterview those previously included in the 1973 survey. The 1977 survey was thus two surveys, one providing cross-sectional sample data suitable for assessing population changes since 1973 and 1969, the other, a panel (or reinterview) study of persons originally interviewed in 1973, allowing the assessment of change for specific, though anonymous, individuals over the period 1973 to 1977. Our report on work schedules is drawn exclusively from the national cross-sectional data of 1977 (Quinn and Staines, 1979).

The topical coverage of the 1977 survey was both similar to and different from its predecessors. In general, the core topics continued to relate to such matters as earnings and fringe benefits, the respondent's task and job content, working hours, job discrimination, job security, etc. Certain topics given a one-time treatment in earlier surveys were deleted or given reduced emphasis. A number of new topics were introduced in the 1977 survey.

The reason for such changes in survey content since 1973, and for similar changes between the 1969 and 1973 surveys, was the desire to limit household interviews with voluntary respondents to an average of eighty minutes. This restriction limits the degree to which a survey of employment, employment conditions, and reactions to employment can be comprehensive, but the restriction is necessary due to cost considerations and the desire to maintain cooperative relationships with respondents.

In the 1969 survey, the special topics concentrated on certain methodological issues, particularly the development of efficient and conceptually sound measures (e.g., of job satisfaction) for continued use. The special supplementary content of the 1973 survey emphasized issues of occupational stress, mental health, and physical health. In 1977, several new topics were introduced, including the employment of the respondent's spouse and the related topic of the impact of employment (particularly work schedules and working hours) on family life. The impetus for including these topics came from the increasing participation of women in the work force and the associated emergence of the dual-earner family as the national norm. To enrich the understanding of this "off-job" aspect of the quality of employment, some questions were added concerning leisure-time use and participation in family and political activities. Other significant topical expansions in 1977 concerned fringe benefits, work hours, unions, job mobility, and worker participation in decisions.

To make room for this new interview material, other topics were dropped or given briefer treatment. The most significant deletions and reductions pertained to work-related health factors, the "importance" ratings of various employment conditions, and a series of topics affecting relatively few workers, such as wage garnishment, effects of automation, and employer interference in workers' privacy.

Overview of the 1977 Cross-Section Sample

A multistage-area probability design was used to select some 2,850 households in seventy-four different geographic areas of the conterminous United States. Eligible respondents (one per household) were sixteen years old or older, currently employed for remuneration for twenty hours or more per week. Of 1,926 chosen persons (many households had no eligible person), 1,515 granted interviews. The net sample therefore included 1,515 respondents representative of all employed adults and drawn from a wide range of occupations and industries. Note the exclusion of important categories: those employed fewer than twenty hours per week; those currently unemployed, unless assured of early return of their usual employment, and those in institutions or otherwise not members of a household.

The term "worker" is used throughout this report to refer to all categories of people working for pay or other monetary gain for at least twenty hours per week. Thus, managers, independent professionals, self-employed business persons, and the like are included along with those who work for an ordinary wage, commission, or salary. Unearned income from investments, transfer payments, pension funds, etc., did not, in itself, disqualify a person as a "worker" for purposes of this survey.

Sample Design

As noted, the 1977 sample was designed to support two studies: a current study of employed persons in the conterminous United States and a panel study of persons originally interviewed in the 1973 Quality of Employment Survey. Although household samples for the two studies might have been selected independently, overlapping samples offered an opportunity for a considerable saving in data collection costs and, quite likely, some increase in the precision of estimated changes from 1973 to 1977. With these objectives in mind, the 1973 sample became the foundation for the 1977 design.

The 1973 sample. The 1973 sample was based on the design frequently used by the Institute for Social Research's Survey Research Center (SRC) for national samples of households in the conterminous United States, exclusive of housing units on military reservations (Kish and Hess, 1965). The SRC definition of housing unit is similar to, but not identical with, the definition developed by the United States Census Bureau (Survey Research Center, 1976). Applied to the 1973 survey, this multistage procedure led to the selection of a sample of 2,788 households in seventy-four geographic areas. Approximately 70 percent of the households had one or more persons who met the eligibility criteria for respondent selection; by an objective procedure, 1,982 persons, one per household, were designated as respondents (Kish, 1949). Of these, 75.5 percent were successfully interviewed.

The implications of selecting only one respondent per household need special emphasis. In households with only one eligible respondent (i.e., one worker), that person was selected as a member of the sample. In households with two eligible respondents (e.g., husband and wife, both working) or more than two, again only one was selected. In short, as the number of eligible respondents in a household rose, the chance that any particular worker in that household would have been selected for the sample declined. Thus the sample contains proportionately more representatives of single-earner households (e.g., husbands and wives who are the sole breadwinners in their households) and fewer representatives of multiple-earner households (e.g., husbands and wives in two-earner households) than the population at large. A weighting scheme, to be described shortly, corrects for this sample imbalance.

The 1977 sample. Interviewers for the 1977 survey returned to the sample listings designated for the 1973 survey. Of necessity, some adjustments were made to sample listings to account for the appearance of new and the disappearance of old residential buildings. The net result was a sample of approximately 2,850 households. Of these, 733 were reported to have no member who met the eligibility criteria. There were 193 housing units where no contact was made with the occupants; consequently, neither household composition nor the eligibility status of household members was determined. At each of the remaining occupied units, by an objective procedure, one eligible person was designated the respondent.[3] Of the 1,926 persons chosen, 1,515 granted interviews. If we assume that about 72 percent of the 193 households not contacted had an eligible person, then the response rate is around 1,515/2,065 or 73.4 percent.

The nonresponse rate of 20 to 30 percent is typical of recent face-to-face interview surveys in the United States. The nonresponse rate is not uniformly distributed throughout the sample, varying from a high of about 50 percent in major cities to a low of about 20 percent elsewhere.

Weighting

Although households were sampled at a constant rate, designated respondents had variable selection rates according to the number of eligible persons within a given household since only one per household was interviewed. For precise representation of the population, the data for each respondent should be weighted by the number of eligibles in the household, including those who were not interviewed. The effects of such a corrective weighting (especially with respect to distributions on sex, age, "collar color," and income level) are great enough to prompt the general use of weighting procedures. The actual number of interviewed respondents in 1977, 1,515, becomes a weighted N of 2,291.

In the analyses that follow, all sample *distributions* including both univariate and bivariate distributions are presented for the weighted sample. However, measures of statistical *relationships* (whether bivariate or multivariate) and tests of statistical *significance*[4] are based on unweighted data because the weighting procedure violates the key statistical assumption of independence of observations.

Analysis Sample

Our analysis is confined to a subset of the total cross-sectional sample of the 1977 Quality of Employment Survey. Specifically, it is restricted to those workers living with a spouse or with a child under eighteen. The unweighted analysis sample is composed of 1,090 workers, divisible into five basic types defined demographically in terms of sex, presence of spouse, and employment status of spouse. The five types are: *sole breadwinning husbands,* men whose wives do not work (N = 477); *dual-earner husbands,* men whose wives do work (N = 274); *sole breadwinning wives,* women whose husbands do not work (N = 41); *dual-earner wives,* women whose husbands do work (N = 226); and *female single parents* with children under eighteen, mothers not living with a spouse (N = 72). Because of their small sample size (N = 6), *male single parents* with children under eighteen, that is, fathers not living with a spouse, are omitted. Compared to the unweighted N of the analysis sample (N = 1,090), the corresponding weighted N is 1,625. In the special analysis of workers from dual-earner couples, the unweighted N is 500.

It should be emphasized that one major (and intended) consequence of this weighting scheme is to restore the five demographic types to their original proportions in the population of workers. For example, most sole breadwinning husbands receive a weight of one, hence their weighted and unweighted Ns scarcely differ; by contrast, most dual-earner husbands and dual-earner wives are assigned a weight of two, hence their weighted N is generally double their unweighted N.[5]

Analysis Strategy: Multiple Regression[6]

Based on ordinary least squares (OLS) estimation procedures, multiple regression provides the basic method of statistical analysis for this study of the effects of work schedules on family life. The advantages of multiple regression include its ability (1) to estimate the effects of many independent variables simultaneously even if such variables are confounded, (2) to assess nonlinear and interactive effects as well as linear and additive ones, and (3) to present results in an informative and interpretable way.

Predictors

Multiple regression readily handles different types of predictors. In particular, it handles nominal predictors (i.e., those based on nominal scales), a category of predictors used extensively in the present analysis. It does so by converting them to dummy variables, each of which has two values, membership in the category versus nonmembership. (For some purposes, continuous measures including those based on ordinal, interval or ratio scales may also be converted to dummy variables.) For example, the first demographic variable (the five types of workers) converts into five dummy variables: sole breadwinning husbands versus all others, dual-earner husbands versus all others, sole breadwinning wives versus all others, dual-earner wives versus all others, and female single parents versus all others. One of the five categories (sole breadwinning husbands) is chosen somewhat arbitrarily as the reference category. In order to avoid linear dependence among the predictors, we omit the reference category from the multiple regressions, meaning that the first demographic variable is represented in the regression equations by four dummy variable terms. The dummy variable strategy applies primarily to two of the three demographic controls (type of worker, family life-cycle stage) and to two of the three work schedule characteristics (pattern of days worked, pattern of hours worked [shift]).

Regression Coefficients

Multiple regression offers us a choice between standardized and nonstandardized regression coefficients. We opt for metric (nonstandardized) regression coefficients for two reasons. First, in our analysis of moderator effects, we compare the slopes of regressions computed for different subgroups of the survey sample. Such comparisons are valid only for metric regression coefficients, since comparing standardized coefficients computed on different subgroups confounds changes in the slope of the regression line with changes in the variance of the independent or dependent variables across these subgroups (Duncan, 1975). Second, the metric regression coefficients are generally quite interpretable. All the major independent variables (e.g., dummy variable measures of worker's shift, number of hours worked per week, etc.) and several of the major dependent variables (e.g., number of hours spent in various family roles) have inherently meaningful metrics.

Curvilinearity

Because of the extensive use made of nominal predictors in this analysis, the issue of curvilinear effects arises infrequently. The only work schedule characteristic measured continuously is number of hours worked each week. We test for nonlinear effects of this predictor by using polynomial regression, which introduces powers of the independent variable into the regression equations. Actually, we introduce only the quadratic (or squared) term in addition to the linear term, thereby testing only for a nonlinear pattern in which there is a single bend in the curve of the relationship between the predictor and criterion. At issue here is whether the quadratic term adds significantly to the variance accounted for by the linear term. More complicated curvilinear patterns as represented by higher-order powers go beyond what is theoretically and substantively meaningful here.

Moderator Effects

The method of moderated regression allows us to include moderator effects (interactive or conditioning effects) within the scope of regression methodology. The essential components of a moderator (or conditioning) effect are a predictor (or, more generally, a set of predictors), a moderator (conditioning) variable, and a criterion. A moderator effect exists when the moderator variable conditions or specifies the effect of the predictor on the criterion, that is, when the slope of the regression of the criterion on the predictor varies significantly across levels of the moderator. Such moderator effects are tested with a regression equation that includes the predictor, the moderator, and all cross-product terms formed by multiplying the predictor by the moderator. The key statistical test here is whether the cross-product term or terms make a significant incremental contribution to variance accounted for, that is, net of the additive (or main) effects of the predictor and moderator variables. Further discussion of the procedures for detecting moderator effects is deferred until later chapters: for the main analysis, until Chapter 5, a chapter devoted solely to moderator effects; and until Chapter 6 for the special analysis of dual-earner couples.

Summary

The entire regression strategy adopted here may be summarized as a sequence of three steps, each addressing a separate statistical question. First, what are the effects of the demographic control variables on the measures of family life? Here we are interested in the regression coefficients for specific control variables and in the total variance accounted for in the case of each dependent variable by the full set of control variables. Second, what are the effects of the work schedule characteristics net of the effects of demographic controls? That is, for each dependent variable, what are the regression coefficients for the various measures of work schedules, including the *quadratic* (or squared) term for number of hours worked, and how much variance does the set of work schedule characteristics contribute net of controls? Third, for each pairing of dependent variable and moderator, which predictors interact with the moderator such that the resulting cross-product term or terms significantly increment the variance explained?

Measures: Items and Distributions

We now detail the measures used in this study and provide *weighted* distributional data on responses to these measures. Where relevant we also provide separate (weighted) distributions by sex. Information appears for three classes of measures: demographic controls, predictors, and dependent variables. Information on a fourth class of measures, moderator variables, is deferred until Chapter 5 on moderator effects. Relevant sections of the interview are presented in Appendix A.

Demographic Controls

Type of worker. Table 3.1 contains weighted distributional data on the five types of workers distinguished earlier on the basis of sex, pres-

TABLE 3.1
Type of Worker[a]

Type of Worker	Number in Sample
Sole Breadwinning Husbands	506 31.1%
Dual-Earner Husbands	513 31.6
Sole Breadwinning Wives	43 2.6
Dual-Earner Wives	475 29.2
Female Single Parents	88 5.4
All types	1625 100[b]

[a]Weighted distribution.
[b]Due to rounding error, percentages in this table and subsequent tables do not always add to exactly 100.

ence of a spouse, and employment status of the spouse. The most frequent types are dual-earner husbands, who represent approximately one-third (31.6 percent) of the total weighted analysis sample (N = 1,625). Close behind are sole breadwinning husbands representing almost another third (31.1 percent), and then dual-earner wives (29.2 percent). The two remaining types are female single parents with 5.4 percent and sole breadwinning wives with 2.6 percent. Sole breadwinning wives, the last and most heterogeneous type in this sample, consist of wives of four categories of men: unemployed, retired, disabled, or students.

Family life-cycle stage. Table 3.2 presents weighted distributions on family life-cycle stage. Because all members of the analysis sample live with either a spouse or child, the majority of workers fall into one of the parental categories of the life cycle. The two childless categories (i.e., no child under eighteen living in the household) contain 14.0 percent of those under forty-five in the analysis sample and 21.1 percent of those forty-five or over. The remaining 64.9 percent are parents, including 27.8 percent who have a preschool child, 23.0 percent whose youngest child is in grade school, and 14.0 percent with an adolescent as their youngest child. The distributions on family life-cycle stage differ little for the two sexes. A slightly larger proportion of working men than working women are forty-five or over and not living

TABLE 3.2
Family Life-Cycle Stage by Sex[a]

| Family Life-Cycle Stage | Worker's Sex | | All Workers |
	Men	Women	
Under 45, No	134	94	228
Children under 18	13.2%	15.5%	14.0%
Youngest Child	289	163	452
under 6	28.4	26.9	27.8
Youngest Child	216	157	373
6–12	21.2	25.9	23.0
Youngest Child	143	85	228
13–17	14.1	14.0	14.0
45 or Older, No	235	107	342
Children under 18	23.1	17.7	21.1
All Stages[b]	1017	606	1623
	62.7	37.3	100

[a]Weighted distribution.
[b]Percents add up to 100 across this row; all others are column percents.

with a child under eighteen, and slightly more women than men report that their youngest child is in grade school.

Education. According to the data on education by sex in Table 3.3, 21.7 percent of the weighted analysis sample completed their schooling without attaining a high school diploma; 39.3 percent have a diploma but no additional education; another 22.3 percent have some college training though not a college degree; and 16.7 percent have achieved a four-year college degree or more. The sexes display slightly different patterns of educational attainment. Working men are somewhat more likely to have completed a college degree, and working women are, conversely, somewhat more likely to have terminated their formal education after achieving a high school diploma.

Predictors (Work Schedule Characteristics)

There is no consensus among investigators as to the best dimensions for describing work schedules. Some research emphasizes the amount as opposed to the scheduling of worktime; other research focuses on the conventionality *or* the regularity of work schedules; still other research concentrates on the distinction between standard hours and overtime. Our preliminary investigations, which included these and other dimensions, led us to select three dimensions (or characteristics) that appear

TABLE 3.3
Level of Formal Education Attained by Sex[a]

Level of Formal Education Attained	Worker's Sex		All Workers
	Men	Women	
Less than a High School Diploma	227 2.4%	123 20.5%	350 21.7%
High School Diploma	372 36.7	263 43.8	635 39.3
Some College Education but No Degree	226 22.3	134 22.3	360 22.3
College Degree or Beyond	189 18.6	81 13.5	270 16.7
All Levels[b]	1014 62.8	601 37.2	1615 100

[a]Weighted distribution.
[b]Percents add up to 100 across this row; all others are column percents.

to capture the most important distinctions among work schedules for a general analysis of individual workers. These are: pattern of days worked each week, pattern of hours worked each day (shift), and number of hours worked each week.[7] Chapter 6 explains how we modify and supplement this list of work schedule characteristics for the special analysis of two-earner couples.

Patterns of days worked and hours worked (shift). We divide the patterns of days worked each week into three categories: (1) a standard pattern in which workers adhere to a fixed (or nonvariable) pattern of days that excludes weekend work (nonvariable weekdays); (2) a nonstandard pattern in which workers work the same days each week but where at least one of those days is a Saturday or Sunday (nonvariable weekend days); and (3) another nonstandard pattern, according to which workers do not work the same days each week (variable days). Similarly, we can divide the pattern of hours worked each day into five categories of shift, one standard and four nonstandard: (1) the day (or standard) shift in which the worker begins work each day between 3:30 a.m. and 11:59 a.m.; (2) the afternoon shift, beginning each day between noon and 7:59 p.m.; (3) the night shift, beginning each day between 8 p.m. and 3:29 a.m.; (4) rotating shifts; and (5) other irregular patterns of hours (variable hours).[8]

Accordingly, weighted distributional data on work schedule characteristics indicate the proportion of workers who work a standard pat-

TABLE 3.4
Shift by Pattern of Days Worked:
All Workers[a]

	Pattern of Days Worked			
Shift	Nonvariable Weekdays	Nonvariable Weekend Days	Variable Days	All Patterns
Day	859	227	75	1161
	85.6%	59.4%	33.6%	72.2%
Afternoon	49	39	14	102
	4.9	10.2	6.3	6.3
Night	13	26	16	55
	1.3	6.8	7.2	3.4
Rotating	11	16	50	77
	1.1	4.2	22.4	4.8
Other	72	74	68	214
	7.2	19.4	30.5	13.3
All Shifts[b]	1004	382	223	1609
	62.4	23.7	13.9	100

[a]Weighted distribution.
[b]Percents add up to 100 across this row; all others are column percents.

tern of days or a standard pattern of hours (day shift) or both. Table 3.4 presents the joint (bivariate) distribution for these two characteristics, with the row and column marginal frequencies representing the univariate distributions for patterns of hours and days, respectively. Tables 3.5 and 3.6 present the same data for men and women, respectively. Most workers (62.4 percent) in the total weighted analysis sample work a regular pattern of weekdays with no weekend work; 23.7 percent work a regular schedule that includes at least one weekend day, and the remaining 13.9 percent report working a variable pattern of days. Almost three-quarters of workers in the sample (72.2 percent) work a (stable) day shift, 6.3 percent work an afternoon shift, 3.4 percent a night shift, 4.8 percent a rotating shift, and the remaining 13.3 percent some other (variable) pattern of hours.

The distributions by sex also hold certain interest. Women are slightly more likely to work a regular pattern of weekdays and men tend to report more weekend work. On the other hand, sex makes very little difference when it comes to shiftwork. Women are just as likely as men to work the afternoon, night or rotating shift.

The joint (bivariate) distribution demonstrates that 53.4 percent of workers have schedules that are standard with respect to both days (nonvariable weekdays) and hours (day shift); 9.0 percent have days

TABLE 3.5

Shift by Pattern of Days Worked:
Men Only[a]

	Pattern of Days Worked			
Shift	Nonvariable Weekdays	Nonvariable Weekend Days	Variable Days	All Patterns
Day	512	173	45	730
	83.0%	66.5%	34.4%	72.4
Afternoon	33	21	3	57
	5.3	8.1	2.3	5.7
Night	11	15	5	31
	1.8	5.8	3.8	3.1
Rotating	8	8	36	52
	1.3	3.1	27.5	5.2
Other	53	43	42	138
	8.6	16.5	32.1	13.7
All Shifts[b]	617	260	131	1008
	61.2	25.8	13.0	100

[a]Weighted distribution.
[b]Percents add up to 100 across this row; all others are column percents.

TABLE 3.6

Shift by Pattern of Days Worked:
Women Only[a]

	Pattern of Days Worked			
Shift	Nonvariable Weekdays	Nonvariable Weekend Days	Variable Days	All Patterns
Day	347	54	30	431
	89.7%	44.3%	32.6%	71.7%
Afternoon	16	18	11	45
	4.1	14.8	12.0	7.5
Night	2	11	11	24
	0.5	9.0	12.0	4.0
Rotating	3	8	14	25
	0.8	6.6	15.2	4.2
Other	19	31	26	76
	4.9	25.4	28.3	12.6
All Shifts[b]	87	122	92	601
	64.4	20.3	15.3	100

[a]Weighted distribution.
[b]Percents add up to 100 across this row; all others are column percents.

that are standard but hours that are not; 18.8 percent have standard hours but nonstandard days; and the remaining 18.8 percent have non-standard schedules in both respects.

Number of hours worked. The third work schedule characteristic, number of hours worked each week, is measured by the following question: "The 'forty-hour' week is a very common term. When people give the hours they work a second thought, however, and start counting the hours up, they sometimes find that they work somewhat more or somewhat less than forty hours. During the average week how many hours do you work, not counting the time you take off for meals?" We present the data on number of hours worked in the form of median values (weighted) and standard deviations (weighted): median = 40.0 hours per week and s.d. = 11.6 hours for the total analysis sample; median = 45.0 hours per week and s.d. = 11.3 hours for employed men; and median = 40.0 hours and s.d. = 10.1 hours for employed women. It is clear from the data that employed men work longer hours than employed women.

Intercorrelations among Predictors[9]

Table 3.7 displays the intercorrelations among measures of work schedule characteristics, based on the total unweighted analysis sample. All the correlations reported here from the table achieve statistical significance at $p < .05$. The table demonstrates that, for the most part, people who work a standard schedule on one work characteristic tend to work a standard schedule on other characteristics. For example, working a regular pattern of days (nonvariable weekdays) correlates positively with working a standard pattern of hours (day shift) ($r = .36$) and correlates negatively with number of hours worked per week ($r = -.30$). Conversely, in line with widely held expectations, regular weekend work is associated with long hours of work ($r = .33$), and working a variable pattern of days is associated with rotating shiftwork ($r = .37$). On the other hand, no strong connection exists between shiftwork and number of hours worked per week. Interestingly, this pattern of associations changes little when recomputed for employed men and employed women separately (data not shown).

Dependent Variables (Measures of Family Life)

Time in family roles. This study employs six major dependent variables. Two concern the amount of time spent in family roles, three refer to work/family conflict and the sixth taps overall family adjustment. All parents in the sample were asked two questions: "On the

TABLE 3.7

Correlations (Pearson r's) among Work
Schedule Characteristics: All Workers (N = 1090)

	Day Shift	Afternoon Shift	Night Shift	Rotating Shift	Other Shift	Number of Hours Worked Per Week
Nonvariable Weekdays	.36**	− .06*	− .10**	− .23**	− .22**	− .30**
Nonvariable Weekend Days	− .12**	.06	.08*	− .04	.09**	.33**
Variable Days	− .35**	.01	.05	.37**	.19**	.02
Day Shift						− .02
Afternoon Shift						− .04
Night Shift						− .06
Rotating Shift						− .04
Other Shift						.11**

*p < .05.
**p < .01.

average, on days when you're working, about how much time do you spend (taking care of or) doing things with your child(ren)?" "And how much time on days when you're not working?" Answers to these two questions and to questions about the pattern of days worked each week formed the basis of an estimate of the average amount of time a respondent spent with his or her children during a week. Similarly, all workers in the sample were asked: "On the average, on days when you're working, about how much time do you spend on home chores — things like cooking, cleaning, repairs, shopping, yardwork, and keeping track of money and bills?" "And about how much time on days when you're not working?" As in the earlier case of parenthood, an estimate was constructed of time spent on home chores during the average week. The questions about home chores were specifically designed to include traditionally male activities (e.g., repairs) as well as traditionally female activities (e.g., cooking) and, likewise, outdoor (e.g., yardwork, shopping) as well as indoor responsibilities (e.g., cleaning). These activities are referred to here generically as "housework."

Workers report spending more time with their children (parents only) than they spend on housework (all workers). The median values (weighted) and standard deviations (weighted) for an average work-week are 21.0 hours and 16.2 hours, respectively, for parental time;

TABLE 3.8
Total Work/Family Conflict by Sex[a]

| Total Conflict | Worker's Sex | | All Workers |
	Men	Women	
A Lot	103	64	167
	10.2%	10.6%	10.3%
Somewhat	241	152	393
	23.8	25.3	24.3
Not Too Much	408	252	660
	40.3	41.9	40.9
Not At All	261	133	394
	25.8	22.1	24.4
All Levels[b]	1013	601	1614
	62.8	37.2	100

[a]Weighted distribution.
[b]Percents add up to 100 across this row; all others are column percents.

and 17.0 hours and 13.9 hours for housework. There is a large difference between the sexes on these time allocations, however. Women
average much more time than men with their children (31.5 versus
16.0 hours per week) and, likewise, much more time on housework
(28.0 versus 11.0 hours per week). Women also display consistently
higher standard deviations than men: 17.0 versus 13.0 hours in the case
of child care and 13.4 versus 9.6 hours in the case of housework.

Work/family conflict. To obtain a measure of total work/family
conflict, interviewers asked all workers living with a family member:
"How much do your job and your family life interfere with each other?
A lot, somewhat, not too much, or not at all?" Respondents answering
"a lot" or "somewhat" were then asked: "In what ways do they interfere
with each other?" A weighted distribution of answers to the first question appears in Table 3.8. About one-third (34.6 percent) of workers
report that their job and their family life interfere with each other
"somewhat" or "a lot," with 10.3 percent opting for the highest level of
interference ("a lot"). Interestingly, this is one case where sex makes
little difference in the pattern of responses.

Two other measures of work/family conflict are based on the follow-
up question about types of conflict (Tables 3.9 and 3.10). Almost one-
sixth of the total weighted sample (16.3 percent) complain about excessive work hours interfering with family life. This measure of "hours
conflict" has three levels: severe (the 5.6 percent who mention hours

TABLE 3.9
Hours Conflict by Sex[a]

| Hours Conflict | Worker's Sex | | All Workers |
	Men	Women	
Severe	65	24	89
	6.5%	4.0%	5.6%
Moderate	126	46	172
	12.5	7.7	10.7
Low	815	525	1340
	81.0	88.2	83.7
All Levels[b]	1006	595	1601
	62.8	37.2	100

[a]Weighted distribution.
[b]Percents add up to 100 across this row; all others are column percents.

TABLE 3.10
Schedule Conflict by Sex[a]

| Schedule Conflict | Worker's Sex | | All Workers |
	Men	Women	
Severe	24	26	50
	2.4%	4.4%	3.1%
Moderate	48	56	104
	4.8	9.4	6.5
Low	934	513	1447
	92.8	86.2	90.4
All Levels[b]	1006	595	1601
	62.8	37.2	100

[a]Weighted distribution.
[b]Percents add up to 100 across this row; all others are column percents.

conflict and who report "a lot" of overall work/family conflict), moderate (the 10.7 percent who likewise mention hours conflict but who report that work and family life interfere with each other only "somewhat"), and low (the remaining workers, who either report only other types of conflict or who do not report that work and family life interfere with each other "a lot" or "somewhat").

Similarly, 9.6 percent of the workers cite one or more scheduling problems. Three levels of "schedule conflict" are distinguished: severe (the 3.1 percent citing schedule conflict and reporting "a lot" of overall work/family conflict), moderate (the 6.5 percent citing schedule conflict but reporting that work and family life interfere with each other "somewhat") and low (those either reporting only other types of conflict or not reporting that work and family life interfere with each other "a lot" or "somewhat"). The types of interference reported do vary appreciably by sex, with employed men more likely than employed women to complain of hours conflict and women more likely than men to mention schedule conflict.

Family adjustment. The index of family adjustment is based on ratings of marital satisfaction, marital happiness, and family satisfaction. The marital items are, obviously, asked only of married respondents; the question about family satisfaction is asked only of parents. Thus, scores on the index of family adjustment represent mean ratings of all three items for married parents, mean ratings of the two marital items for persons married but currently childless, and ratings of family satisfaction for female single parents. The wordings of the three items are as follows: "All in all, how satisfied would you say you are with your marriage?" "Taking everything together, how happy would you say your marriage is?" "All in all, how satisfied would you say you are with your family life?" These three items measuring family adjustment have parallel response options: Extremely satisfied/extremely happy, very satisfied/very happy, somewhat satisfied/somewhat happy, not too satisfied/not too happy.

As Tables 3.11–3.13 make clear, distributions of responses are heavily skewed in a negative direction (i.e., mostly positive responses) for all three rating scales, most noticeably for marital satisfaction and least so for family satisfaction. Separated by sex, the data on family adjustment show that working men offer appreciably more positive assessments of their family life than working women. For each of the three items measuring adjustment, at least 10 percent more men than women score in the uppermost (most favorable) category. The index of family adjustment displays a high level of internal reliability (coefficient alpha = .86). As expected, the two items tapping the quality of the marital relationship (marital satisfaction, marital happiness) are more closely related to each other ($r = .79$) than they are to the question about satisfaction with family life ($r = .64$ and $r = .58$, respectively).

Intercorrelations among Dependent Variables

As noted earlier, we may divide the six measures of family life into three categories: those concerning the amount of time invested in family roles (parenting and housework), those tapping work/family

TABLE 3.11
Marital Satisfaction by Sex[a]

| Marital Satisfaction | Worker's Sex | | All Workers |
	Men	Women	
Extremely Satisfied	497 49.3%	189 37.1%	686 45.2%
Very Satisfied	419 41.5	242 47.5	661 43.5
Somewhat Satisfied	79 7.8	68 13.4	147 9.7
Not Too Satisfied	14 1.4	10 2.0	24 1.6
All Levels[b]	1009 66.5	509 33.5	1518 100

[a]Weighted distribution.
[b]Percents add up to 100 across this row; all others are column percents.

TABLE 3.12
Marital Happiness by Sex[a]

| Marital Happiness | Worker's Sex | | All Workers |
	Men	Women	
Extremely Happy	443 44.1%	172 33.9%	615 40.7%
Very Happy	442 42.0	262 51.6	684 45.2
Somewhat Happy	123 12.3	69 13.6	192 12.7
Not Too Happy	16 1.6	5 1.0	21 1.4
All levels[b]	1004 66.4	508 33.6	1512 100

[a]Weighted distribution.
[b]Percents add up to 100 across this row; all others are column percents.

conflict, and the index of family adjustment. Intercorrelations among members of each of the first two categories are of interest, as are correlations between representatives of the three different categories. Correlations involving time spent with children are, of necessity, based on only those workers who live with a child under eighteen. Again, all correlations reported are significant at p < .05.

TABLE 3.13
Satisfaction with Family Life by Sex[a]

| Satisfaction with Family Life | Worker's Sex | | All Workers |
	Men	Women	
Extremely Satisfied	209	80	289
	32.2%	20.0%	27.6%
Very Satisfied	342	218	560
	52.7	54.5	53.4
Somewhat Satisfied	87	83	170
	13.4	20.8	16.2
Not Too Satisfied	11	19	30
	1.7	4.8	2.9
All Levels[b]	649	400	1049
	61.9	38.1	100

[a]Weighted distribution.
[b]Percents add up to 100 across this row; all others are column percents.

According to Table 3.14, for the total (unweighted) analysis sample, time spent with children is substantially correlated with time spent on housework ($r = .42$) (cf., $r = .38$ reported by Bohen and Viveros-Long, 1981). For clearly artifactual reasons that concern the construction of the measures, total work/family conflict correlates positively and substantially with reports of the two major types of interference, hours conflict and schedule conflict ($r = .59$ and $.41$, respectively). Nonetheless, these two specific modes of interference are not themselves related for the total analysis sample.

As for correlations between the three categories of the dependent variables, total work/family conflict is negatively correlated with amount of time spent with children ($r = -.16$) but not with time on housework. Moreover, whereas reports of hours conflict correlate negatively with time allotted to both family roles ($r = -.18$ for child care and $r = -.12$ for housework), reports of schedule conflict are somewhat *positively* correlated with amount of time spent on housework ($r = .06$). The index of family adjustment correlates negatively with total work/family conflict ($r = -.14$) and reports of schedule conflict ($r = -.10$) but does not correlate with any of the other variables.

Sex makes an appreciable difference to a number of the correlations. The positive correlation between time allocated to children and to housework ($r = .42$), for example, proves much weaker when calculated separately for fathers ($r = .25$) and for mothers ($r = .23$), pre-

TABLE 3.14

Correlations (Pearson r's) among Family Measures

	Family Measures				
	Time in Housework	Total Conflict	Hours Conflict	Schedule Conflict	Family Adjustment
All Workers (N = 1090)					
Time in Child Care	.42**	− .16**	− .18**	.02	.02
Time in Housework		− .02	− .12**	.06*	− .04
Total Conflict			.59**	.41**	− .14**
Hours Conflict				.04	− .05
Schedule Conflict					− .10**
Men (N = 751)					
Time in Child Care	.25**	− .19**	− .15**	− .04	.18**
Time in Housework		− .04	− .12**	.03	.07
Total Conflict			.64**	.36**	− .15**
Hours Conflict				.11**	− .11**
Schedule Conflict					− .05
Women (N = 339)					
Time in Child Care	.23**	− .21**	−.17**	− .03	.09
Time in Housework		− .04	.00	− .01	.11*
Total Conflict			.46**	.52**	− .13*
Hours Conflict				− .07	.04
Schedule Conflict					− .14*

*p<.05.
**p<.01.

sumably because the ranges of the two variables are much attenuated when only one sex is involved. On the other hand, the essentially zero correlation between parental time and family adjustment becomes positive for each sex taken separately, significantly so for fathers (r = .18); likewise, the near zero correlation between time in housework and family adjustment also becomes positive for the two sexes taken on their own, significantly so in the case of women (r = .11). It seems likely that for these two latter correlations between time in family roles and family adjustment, the variance contributed by between-sex (mean) differences in family time obscures the within-sex correlations.

Notes

1. Much of this account of the study's methodology is adapted from Quinn and Staines (1979).
2. The change in name does not reflect any major change in purpose. The term "working conditions" misled some people because of its unintended emphasis on physical surroundings.
3. The respondent selection procedure, while basically the same as in 1973, was varied in

households that included a 1973 respondent who was also a member of the current study population. If no eligible household member was a respondent in the earlier survey, the selection process was identical with the 1973 procedure. If a currently eligible household member was interviewed in 1973, the alternate procedure was: (1) classify eligible persons as "old" or "new" according to their eligibility status in 1973; (2) using the objective respondent selection procedure, choose one eligible person; (3) if the selected person is "new," accept that individual as the designated respondent; (4) if the selected person is "old," the 1973 respondent is also the 1977 designated respondent.

4. Standard tests of statistical significance are not strictly appropriate here because they assume simple random sampling. The present multistage-area probability design generates standard errors somewhat larger than those based on simple random sampling. Thus, the direction of the design effect is to increase the probability of Type 1 errors. Fortunately, the design effect is close to unity in the present case (Quinn and Staines, 1979). Hence, because the design effect is small and because no simple way exists to make precise adjustments, significance testing based on simple random sampling is adopted here as a convenient approximation.

5. Some dual-earner husbands and dual-earner wives receive a weight of only one, however. This apparent anomaly arises when the spouse of the worker in question works fewer than twenty hours per week and thus fails to meet the study's eligibility requirement. Such cases are treated as dual-earner couples in the study's analyses but the spouse who works part-time does not add to the weight assigned to the household.

Conversely, in those households in which someone other than the husband or wife also works for pay, it is possible for sole breadwinning spouses to receive a weight greater than one and for dual-earner spouses to receive a weight greater than two.

6. This account of regression methodology is based largely on discussions by Cohen and Cohen (1975) and by House and his colleagues (House, 1980; Larocco et al., 1980).

7. Unless otherwise specified, all measures of work schedule characteristics refer to a worker's main job.

8. Little consensus exists in previous research as to how the various shifts should be defined. The Bureau of Labor Statistics to take one example, distinguishes between four different categories: two types of late shift (evening shift and night shift), miscellaneous shift, and day schedule. Late shifts are defined according to whether half the hours scheduled fall between 4:00 p.m. and midnight (evening shift) or between midnight and 8:00 a.m. (night shift). All schedules of fewer than six or more than twelve hours per day are placed in the miscellaneous category. The day schedule designates those work schedules in which at least half the hours fall between 8:00 a.m. and 4:00 p.m. (Hedges and Sekscenski, 1979). Studies of particular work organizations introduce idiosyncratic interpretations of shifts. Mott et al. (1965), for instance, studied five plants at two companies. In the first company, the three fixed shifts (day, afternoon, and night) began at 8:00 a.m., 4:00 p.m., and midnight, respectively, and each lasted eight hours. In the second company, all shifts began one hour earlier, again at eight-hour intervals. Patterns of rotating shifts evidenced even greater variation between companies.

9. Missing data were deleted "pairwise" rather than "listwise" in the computation of all correlations. That is, each correlation was computed across all cases with valid data on both variables involved, regardless of whether information was missing on some of these cases for other correlations in the same analysis. In addition, all tests of the statistical significance of correlations are two-tailed.

4

The Main Effects of Work Schedules on Family Life

In most analyses based on multiple regression, results for demographic controls hold little interest compared to results for the major predictors. In our case, however, a considerable body of literature exists regarding the relationship between demographic variables and family life. Accordingly, this chapter presents the data relating demographics to family measures. These data are substantively significant and merit more than the usual perfunctory consideration, yet are still secondary in importance to the data connecting work schedules to family life.

Correlations between Predictors (Demographic Controls, Work Schedule Characteristics) and Dependent Variables (Measures of Family Life)

Table 4.1 presents bivariate correlations between demographic control variables and measures of family life. The table contains a substantial number of significant correlations, including several that are particularly large. Being in one of the categories of employed women tends to be correlated with longer hours in the two family roles (parenting and housework) and with more frequent reports of schedule conflict. At this zero-order level, interestingly, working women score no higher (or lower) than working men on total work/family conflict. The correlations based on family life-cycle stage indicate that childless workers tend to experience less interference between work and family life and to report higher family adjustment than working parents.

TABLE 4.1

Correlations (Pearson r's) between Demographic Controls
and Family Measures: All Workers (N = 1090)

Demographic Controls	Family Measures					
	Time in Child Care	Time in Housework	Total Conflict	Hours Conflict	Schedule Conflict	Family Adjustment
Sole Breadwinning Husbands	-.30**	-.38**	0	.04	-.07*	.14**
Dual-Earner Husbands	-.11**	-.19**	-.02	.06	-.03	.05
Sole Breadwinning Wives	.05	.15**	-.03	-.04	-.02	-.04
Dual-Earner Wives	.28**	.47**	.01	-.04	.06*	-.03
Female Single Parents	.25**	.19**	.03	-.09**	.11**	-.28**
Childless, under 45	–	-.06*	.02	.02	.02	.08*
Youngest Child under 6	.20**	.03	.14**	.06	.10**	0
Youngest Child 6–12	0	.09**	.03	.05	-.01	-.06*
Youngest Child 13–17	-.26**	-.03	.03	-.02	-.04	-.08**
Childless, 45 or Older	–	-.05	-.22**	-.12**	-.08*	.07
Education	-.09*	-.03	.08**	.05	-.04	.05

*p < .05.
**p < .01.

TABLE 4.2

Correlations (Pearson r's) between Work Schedule Characteristics
and Family Measures: All Workers (N = 1090)

Work Schedule Characteristics	Family Measures					
	Time in Child Care	Time in Housework	Total Conflict	Hours Conflict	Schedule Conflict	Family Adjustment
Nonvariable Weekdays	.17**	.09**	-.19**	-.16**	-.17**	.05
Nonvariable Weekend Days	-.14**	-.17**	.13**	.18**	.08**	-.01
Variable Days	-.06	.08*	.10**	.01	.14**	-.06*
Day Shift	-.02	-.08**	-.20**	-.10**	-.21**	.03
Afternoon Shift	.12**	.14**	.11**	.02	.23**	-.06*
Night Shift	.05	.06	.07*	.02	.10**	-.02
Rotating Shift	-.01	.07*	.08**	.04	.10**	.04
Other Shift	-.07	-.05	.08**	.07*	-.01	-.02
Number of Hours Worked	-.36**	-.38**	.25**	.32**	0	.07*

*p < .05.
**p < .01.

Among employed parents, moreover, those with preschoolers spend the most time with their children and encounter the highest level of total work/family conflict. In addition, a worker's level of education is negatively correlated with time spent with children and positively correlated with total work/family conflict.

In analyzing the significant bivariate correlations between work schedule characteristics and measures of family life (Table 4.2), we begin with the working assumption on which this study's hypotheses are based: that traditionally favored schedules (i.e., regular pattern of days without weekend work, day shift, and modest number of hours worked per week) are associated with favorable family outcomes (i.e., extended time in family roles, low work/family interference, and high family adjustment). In line with this working assumption and with only one exception, nonstandard patterns of days (especially regular weekend work) are negatively correlated with measures of the quality of family life. Working a nonday shift is generally correlated positively with total work/family conflict; yet, surprisingly, in a number of instances it is also correlated *positively* with amount of time spent in family roles. Finally, as expected, number of hours worked each week correlates negatively with time spent in family roles and positively with measures of work/family interference; yet, quite unexpectedly, it correlates positively with family adjustment.

In sum, most but not all of the significant zero-order correlations in Table 4.1 between demographic controls and measures of family life conform to our general expectations; likewise, most but not all of the significant correlations in Table 4.2 conform to our working assumption about the relationship between nonstandard work schedules and the quality of family life. For a number of reasons, however, zero-order correlations offer an incomplete assessment of the effects of demographic controls and work schedule characteristics on measures of family life. In the first place, the intercorrelations within each set of predictors (demographic controls, work schedule characteristics) make it difficult to see their independent effects and may actually suppress some of the zero-order correlations between predictors and criteria. Similarly, correlations between demographic controls and work schedule characteristics may either inflate or suppress the true effects of each on family life. Moreover, since the different dimensions of family life may be affected by multiple work schedule characteristics as well as by the various demographic controls, a measure of the cumulative effects of the various sets of predictors is needed. Finally, the Pearson correlations in Tables 4.1 and 4.2 reflect only linear relations among variables, and it is possible that in the case of one work schedule characteristics, namely number of hours worked per week, the effects on family life are curvilinear.

Multivariate Main Effects

Multiple regression offers a way to overcome these problems. It permits us to regress each of the six measures of family life on measures of the three demographic control variables and the three work schedule characteristics, allowing where appropriate for curvilinear as well as linear effects of work schedule characteristics on family life.

Demographic Controls

We begin our account of the regression data with the less important (though interesting) set of predictors, namely, the demographic controls. As revealed in the multiple regressions summarized statistically in Table 4.3 and verbally in Tables 4.4 and 4.5, the data concerning the effects of the demographic controls on family measures contain some expected findings as well as some surprising ones.

As noted earlier, the first demographic control variable distinguishes five types of workers based on their sex, the presence of a spouse, and the employment status of the spouse. In presenting the findings on type of worker, we use sole breadwinning husbands as the reference category. Table 4.3 indicates that female single parents spend the most time with their children (15.4 hours more per week than sole breadwinning husbands), followed by dual-earner wives (12.3 hours more) and then sole breadwinning wives (7.9 hours more); next are dual-earner husbands (2.9 hours more), and sole breadwinning husbands report the least parental time. In short, as expected, mothers spend considerably more time with their children than do fathers. Among mothers, single parents register the greatest parental time, presumably because they have no spouse with whom to share the responsibility; and among fathers, dual-earner husbands invest more time in parenting than do sole breadwinning husbands.

In the case of time spent on housework, dual-earner wives report the most time (16.1 hours more per week than sole breadwinning husbands), followed by sole breadwinning wives (14.7 hours more), female single parents (11.5 hours more), dual-earner husbands (1.7 hours more) and, then, sole breadwinning husbands. Thus, in line with the earlier findings on time spent with children and with other investigations of sex differences in the division of labor in families, employed

TABLE 4.3

Metric Regression Coefficients for Net Additive (Linear and Curvilinear) Effects of Work Schedule Characteristics on Family Measures

Demographic Controls and Work Schedule Characteristics (Indep. Var.)	Family Measures (Dep. Var.)					
	Time in Child Care	Time in Housework	Total Conflict	Hours Conflict	Schedule Conflict	Family Adjustment
Demographic Controls						
Type of Worker						
Dual-Earner Husbands	2.921*	1.713*	.024	.049	.018	-.071
Female Single Parents	15.390**	11.510**	.271*	-.094	.195**	-.822**
Dual-Earner Wives	12.320**	16.149**	.246**	.041	.101**	-.169**
Sole Breadwinning Wives	7.924*	14.686**	.246	.053	.028	.289*
(Omitted Category: Sole Breadwinning Husbands)						
Family Life-Cycle Stage						
Youngest Child under 6	—a	5.255**	.146	.012	.009	-.126
Youngest Child 6–12	-5.272**	5.788**	.024	.023	-.027	-.181*
Youngest Child 13–17	-13.049**	3.204*	.037	-.052	-.051	-.204*
Childless, 45 or Older	—a	3.471**	-.339**	-.148*	-.053	-.061
(Omitted Category: Childless, under 45)						
Education	-.763*	.093	.023	.004	-.006	.018
Work Schedule Characteristics						
Days						
Nonvariable Weekend Days	-3.443*	-2.637**	.102	.089*	.082*	-.076
Variable Days	-4.374*	.573	.094	-.024	.133**	-.175*
(Omitted Category: Non-variable Weekdays)						

TABLE 4.3 (Continued)

Demographic Controls and Work Schedule Characteristics (Indep. Var.)	Family Measures (Dep. Var.)					
	Time in Child Care	Time in Housework	Total Conflict	Hours Conflict	Schedule Conflict	Family Adjustment
Shift						
Afternoon	3.522	6.088**	.503**	.088	.397**	−.104
Night	3.296	4.182*	.413**	.106	.226**	.019
Rotating	2.283	4.817**	.430**	.168*	.132*	.201
Other	.154	.392	.204*	.054	.024	−.025
(Omitted Category: Day Shift)						
Number of Hours Worked (linear)	−.271	−.452**	.035**	.010	.004	.003
(quadratic)	.000	.000	.000	.000	.000	.000
Adjusted R² Explained By						
Demographic Controls	.277	.349	.043	.025	.024	.095
Work Schedule Characteristics, Net of Demographic Controls	.047	.062	.107	.097	.082	.005
All Variables	.324	.411	.150	.122	.106	.100
Adjusted Multiple R	.569	.641	.387	.349	.325	.316
N	644	996	1045	1036	1036	1046

*p < .05.
**p < .01.
aFor time in child care, those without children are excluded from the analysis and the omitted category becomes parents whose youngest child is under 6.

TABLE 4.4
Summary of Major Multivariate Main Effects of
Demographic Controls on Family Measures

Family Variables (Dep. Var.)	Demographic Controls (Indep. Var.)		
	Types of Workers		
	Between Sexes	*Within Men*	*Within Women*
Time in Child Care	Mothers > Fathers	Dual-Earner Fathers higher	Single Parents highest
Time in Housework	Women > Men	Dual-Earner Husbands higher	Dual-Earner Wives highest
Total Conflict	Women > Men		
Family Adjustment	Men > Women		Single Parents lowest
	Family Life-Cycle Stage		
Time in Child Care	Younger Children > Older Children		
Time in Housework	Children under 13 > Youngest Child 13–17		
Total Conflict	Nonparents 45 or Over lowest		
Family Adjustment	Youngest Child 7–17 lowest		
	Education		
Time in Child Care	Negative Relationship		

TABLE 4.5
Summary of Major Multivariate Main Effects of
Work Schedule Characteristics on Family Measures

Family Variables (Dep. Var.)	Work Schedule Characteristics (Indep. Var.)
	Days Worked
Time in Child Care	Nonvariable Weekdays > Nonvariable Weekend Days (by 3½ hours/week)
	Nonvariable Weekdays > Variable Days (by 4⅓ hours/week)
Time in Housework	Nonvariable Weekdays > Nonvariable Weekend Days (by 2⅔ hours/week)
Family Adjustment	Nonvariable Weekdays > Variable Days
	Shift
Time in Housework	Shiftwork higher (by approx. 5 hours/week)
Total Conflict	Shiftwork higher
	Number of Hours Worked
Time in Housework	Negative Relationship
Total Conflict	Positive Relationship

women spend considerably more time on housework than do employed men. Unlike the earlier findings on parental time, however, dual-earner wives and sole breadwinning wives report greater time commitment to housework than do female single parents, probably because the latter have no husband to share time with their children. Yet, once again, dual-earner husbands score higher than sole breadwinning husbands on a measure of participation in family life.[1]

In an important departure from the zero-order correlational findings, the regression analyses show that women register greater total work/family conflict than do men. That is, when one controls statistically for the fact that women's work schedules are less demanding than those of men, the greater sensitivity of women to work/family interference emerges clearly.[2] Moreover, although the five types of workers fail to differ significantly on one category of work/family conflict (hours conflict), the other type of problem (schedule conflict) is notably higher for two of the groups of women, single parents and dual-earner wives. Also evident from the table and worth emphasizing is the lower family adjustment of women, especially single parents.

We can summarize the foregoing data on type of worker as follows: Employed women spend more time with their children than do employed men; they also spend more time on housework, experience more work/family conflict, especially of the schedule variety, and register lower family adjustment. Among employed women, moreover, single parents spend the most time with children and experience the most work/family interference and the lowest family adjustment. Among employed men, dual-earner husbands spend more time on child care and housework than do sole breadwinning husbands.

Previous investigation of time use, including studies based on the highly sophisticated methodology of time diaries, address some of these contrasts among types of workers. Precise comparisons of time use reported in different studies are not possible, however, because of technical differences between the regressions used here, which include multivariate controls on work schedules, and the analyses performed elsewhere. Still, comparisons at a general level are informative. Existing research, for example, confirms that working women spend more time with their children and more time on housework than do working men (Meissner et al., 1975, Walker and Woods, 1976) but such research does not consistently show more time spent on child care and housework by dual-earner husbands compared to sole breadwinning husbands (Meissner et al., 1975; Pleck, 1981; ibid, in press; Robinson, 1977; Walker and Woods, 1976).

Previous research also explores sex differences in sensitivity to work/

family conflict. Although such research does not use multivariate analytic techniques, it tends to indicate a greater sensitivity to conflict on the part of women. Keith and Schafer (1980) report that, at the zero-order level, women in two-job families experience significantly more work/family strain than men; and Bohen and Viveros-Long (1981) report that, again at the zero-order level, employed women score significantly higher than employed men on one index of work/family conflict but not on a second index.

Family life-cycle stage represents a second major demographic control in this study. According to the regression data, time spent with children declines as the age of the youngest child increases. The largest amount of parental time is reported by parents of preschoolers. By comparison, those with a child in grade school spend 5.3 hours fewer each week, and those with an adolescent child spend 13.0 hours fewer. Time spent on housework is greatest when the youngest child is under thirteen. Compared to workers under forty-five who have no children, parents of preschoolers report spending 5.3 hours more per week on housework, parents of children in grade school report 5.8 hours more, and parents of adolescents report 3.2 hours more. Family life-cycle stage has only one effect on total work/family conflict: workers forty-five or over who have no children report very little interference. This same group of workers offer the fewest complaints of hours conflict. No differences emerge among the family life-cycle groups on reports of schedule conflict, but workers whose youngest child is between seven and seventeen report the lowest level of family adjustment. We point out here that the parents of preschool children do *not* register the lowest level of family adjustment, as might be expected.

To summarize the data on family life-cycle stage, parents of preschoolers spend the most time with their children and a lot of time on housework. Parents whose youngest child is between seven and seventeen report the lowest level of family adjustment. Childless workers aged forty-five or above record the lowest level of work/family interference, especially on the issue of hours conflict, whereas childless workers under forty-five spend the least amount of time on housework. Other studies have confirmed that parents do more housework than nonparents (Farkas, 1976; Meissner et al., 1975). They have also shown that mothers perform more child care when children are younger (i.e., the time spent on child care lessens as the children get older) but there is no consistent evidence that child-care time lessens for fathers as children get older (Hill and Stafford, 1980; Robinson, 1977; Walker and Woods, 1976).

The third and final demographic control variable is highest level of education attained. Interestingly, education relates significantly to only one of the measures of family life: better educated workers report spending less time with their children. Existing literature on the relationship between education and time spent on child care fails to provide a clearcut point of comparison. Even though previous studies typically report their data separately by sex, their findings appear to lack empirical consistency (Gronau, 1976; Hill and Stafford, 1980; Leibowitz, 1974; Pleck, in press; Robinson, 1977; Walker and Woods, 1976).

Work Schedule Characteristics

Pattern of days worked. Work schedule characteristics represent the set of predictors of greatest interest in the analyses based on multiple regression. Our review of the regression data on work schedule characteristics starts from the earlier working assumption that nonstandard work schedules are negatively related to the quality of family life. As indicated in Chapter 1, four hypotheses derive from this assumption; the first three concern the multivariate main effects of work schedules on family life.

According to the first hypothesis, working a nonstandard pattern of days each week (weekend work, variable days) is negatively related to the quality of the worker's family life. Our findings support this initial hypothesis. The data on patterns of days worked show that, compared to a regular schedule of days which excludes Saturdays and Sundays, a regular schedule that includes weekend work is associated with 3.4 hours fewer per week spent with children and 2.6 hours fewer spent on housework. Regular weekend work is also linked to more frequent reports of hours conflict and schedule conflict but not to greater total work/family conflict. Again based on the regression data, working a variable pattern of days is associated with less time spent with one's children (4.4 hours fewer per week) than working a regular, nonweekend schedule. Having a variable pattern of days, nonetheless, has no significant bearing on the amount of time devoted to housework. No relationship emerges between a variable pattern of days and either total work/family conflict or specific complaints about hours conflict, although the variable schedule is accompanied by more frequent reports of schedule conflict. Not unexpectedly, workers on a variable schedule of days report lower levels of family adjustment. In short, the two major departures from a regular schedule of days (regular weekend work and variable days) tend to be associated with less time in family roles, more work/family interference and, in one instance, lower family adjustment.

Shift. The second hypothesis states that working a nonstandard pattern of hours each day (afternoon, night, or rotating shift; variable hours) is negatively related to the quality of the worker's family life. The regression data linking shiftwork and family life provide only partial support for this hypothesis. The overall pattern is that nonday shifts permit *more* time on housework, yet also *more* work/family conflict. For example, workers on an afternoon shift spend 6.1 hours more each week on housework than do workers on a day shift; they also report more total work/family interference and more schedule conflict. Similarly, workers on a night shift report more time on housework than day shiftworkers (4.2 hours more per week) and higher levels of total work/family conflict and schedule conflict. The pattern for workers on rotating shifts is virtually the same: 4.8 hours more per week on housework and elevated levels of total work/family interference, hours conflict and schedule conflict. By comparison, working some "other" shift, the residual category, is significantly associated with greater total work/family conflict but not with anything else.

To reiterate, the regression data establish that the major nonday shifts tend to be associated with *more* time spent on housework and *more* work/family conflict, especially of the schedule variety. The present data on conflict are thus consistent with the findings from published studies as summarized in Chapter 1. Both present and previous data, that is, document an empirical link between shiftwork and increments in work/family interference, although our data explore the connection in a more comprehensive way.

These data on shiftwork and family life point up the important distinction between amount of time in family roles and scheduling of that time. Contrary to popular conception, shiftwork does not detract from the amount of time workers spend in family roles; in fact, shiftworkers spend more time than other workers on housework. The problems that shiftwork poses for family life concern the scheduling of available time. Apparently, the time that shiftworkers have available for family roles comes at the wrong period of the day; that is, schedules of family members fail to mesh, hence workers' reports of schedule conflict.

The question as to why shiftworkers report spending more time on housework than other workers also deserves consideration. This extra time on housework may derive in part from the fact that people who work at night (i.e., those on night and rotating shifts) have been shown in other studies to sleep from one to two hours fewer per night (i.e., at least five to ten hours fewer per week) than daytime workers (Carpentier and Cazamian, 1977; Zalusky, 1978). In addition, housework includes many solitary activities whose scheduling is highly flexible;

thus, workers whose shifts preclude their spending time in regularly scheduled family activities may view housework as the family role to which they can most reasonably allocate their available time.

Number of hours worked. According to the third hypothesis, working a large number of hours each week is negatively related to the quality of the worker's family life. In our data, nevertheless, number of hours worked each week produces significant relationships with only two of the measures of family life. A high number of hours worked is associated with less time on housework and, in line with existing studies as summarized in Chapter 2, with higher levels of total work/family conflict. In addition, because the number of hours worked each week is the only work schedule characteristic measured on a continuous rather than a categorical scale, it is the only predictor for which a curvilinear relationship with the dependent variables is possible. In no instance, however, do the regression data establish a significant quadratic effect (i.e., squared term) for the number of hours worked. In short, insofar as number of hours worked is associated with the various measures of family life, the relationships appear to be strictly linear.

By way of review of findings relevant to the first three hypotheses, Table 4.6 compares data from this and other studies, both bivariate and multivariate, on the main effects of work schedules on measures of the quality of family life. Given the many technical differences among the various analyses and studies, the high degree of empirical agreement commands attention. According to all sources of data represented in the table, shiftwork is associated with increased work/family conflict, and many hours of work are accompanied by both reduced time in family roles and greater work/family interference. Table 4.6 also documents a number of new findings generated by this study, that is, findings that have no direct analogue in previous investigations. Specifically, our data show that regular weekend work is associated with reduced time in family roles; working a variable pattern of days is accompanied by lower family adjustment; and shiftworkers spend more time than other workers on housework. Finally, in no instance does this study fail to find relationships between work schedule characteristics and family measures that have consistently appeared in earlier research.

Multiple R^2

We conclude our review of the multivariate main effects by considering the amount of variance of the six measures of family life accounted for by the various combinations of predictors in the regressions

TABLE 4.6

Comparisons between Present and Previous Studies of Relationships
between Work Schedule Characteristics and Family Measures

| | FAMILY TIME | | | |
| | Bivariate Analysis | | Multivariate Analysis | |
	Present Study	Previous Studies	Present Study	Previous Studies
Weekend Work	Negative	—	Negative	—
Variable Days	Positive (housework only)	—	Negative (child care only)	—
Shiftwork	Positive	—	Positive (housework only)	—
Number of Hours Worked	Negative	Negative (primarily housework)	Negative (housework only)	—

| | WORK-FAMILY CONFLICT | | | |
| | Bivariate Analysis | | Multivariate Analysis | |
	Present Study	Previous Studies	Present Study	Previous Studies
Weekend Work	Positive	—	ns	—
Variable Days	Positive	—	ns	—
Shiftwork	Positive	Positive	Positive	Positive
Number of Hours Worked	Positive	Positive	Positive	Positive

| | FAMILY ADJUSTMENT | | | |
| | Bivariate Analysis | | Multivariate Analysis | |
	Present Study	Previous Studies	Present Study	Previous Studies
Weekend Work	ns	—	ns	—
Variable Days	Negative	—	Negative	—
Shiftwork	Negative (afternoon shift only)	Negative	ns	—
Number of Hours Worked	Positive	ns	ns	ns

(Table 4.3). The demographic controls constitute our first set of predictors. For these control variables, the multiple R^2 (adjusted) is highest for time spent on housework (.349) and parental time (.277); otherwise it is quite low. The pattern changes substantially, however,

for the variance accounted for by the set of work schedule characteristics net of demographic controls. The value of incremental R^2
(adjusted) is greatest for the measures of work/family interference
(.107 for total conflict, .097 for reports of hours conflict, and .082 for
reports of schedule conflict), substantially lower for measures of time
in family roles (.047 for parental time and .062 for time on housework), and essentially zero for family adjustment. In short, the demographic controls (two of which directly involve family composition) are
effective predictors of time spent in family roles (parenting and housework) while the work schedule characteristics are most effective as
predictors of interference between work and family life. The multiple
R^2 for the total set of predictors (demographic controls plus work
schedule characteristics) follows the pattern established for the demographic control variables taken on their own: highest for time spent on
housework and time with one's children.

Summary

This chapter analyzes the main effects of work schedules on family
life. It also examines relationships between demographic controls and
family measures and finds a number of interesting associations. However, these relationships are held to be of secondary significance. The
chapter draws on both bivariate and multivariate analyses but stresses
the multivariate findings. It begins with the working assumption that
traditionally preferred work schedules (i.e., regular pattern of days
without weekend work, day shift, and modest number of hours worked
per week) are associated with favorable family outcomes (i.e., extended
time in family roles, low work/family conflict, and high family adjustment). This working assumption generates three testable hypotheses.

According to the first hypothesis, working a nonstandard pattern of
days each week (weekend work, variable days) is negatively related to
family life. In line with this initial hypothesis, the multivariate analyses demonstrate that nonstandard days are associated with less time in
family roles, higher levels of specific types of work/family conflict and,
in one instance, lower family adjustment.

The second hypothesis contends that shiftwork is negatively associated with family life. Here, the relevant data paint a more complicated picture. Under multivariate control, shiftwork is associated with
more rather than less time in one family role (housework), a result that
runs counter to this hypothesis. In line with the hypothesis, shiftwork is
associated with more work/family interference. In short, it appears
that the problems created by shiftwork concern the scheduling (or

timing) of family activities rather than the total amount of time available for family activities.

The third hypothesis claims that long working hours are negatively related to family life. The data from the multiple regressions identify only two relationships between number of hours worked and family life, but both relationships support this hypothesis. Specifically, number of hours worked each week is negatively related to time spent on housework and positively related to total work/family interference.

Some of these relationships (shiftwork and number of hours) have also been investigated in other studies. The relevant empirical comparisons have established general agreement between these and previous findings.

In this chapter we also consider amount of variance explained in the case of each of the six family measures. With demographic controls and work schedule characteristics as the combined set of predictors, (adjusted) multiple R^2 is higher for time spent in family roles than for the other dependent variables. Moreover, in the case of time in family roles and family adjustment, demographic controls account for more variance than do work schedule characteristics. For the three measures of work/family conflict, however, work schedule characteristics contribute more of the variance than do the controls.

Notes

1. Though in essential agreement with two earlier reports based on the same dataset (Pleck and Lang, 1978; Pleck, 1981), this report on the effects of wife's employment on husband's time contribution to family roles supercedes the two earlier accounts of the data.

2. The data reported in Chapter 3 indicate that men's work schedules are more demanding than those of women in at least two basic respects: employed men are more likely than employed women to work regularly on weekends and employed men average longer hours each week than employed women. The fact that one needs to control statistically on dimensions of work schedules in order to demonstrate differential sensitivities of men and women to total work/family conflict also explains why, in an earlier analysis of these data, Pleck et al., (1980) found that sex and total conflict were unrelated at the zero-order level and that female single parents registered less total conflict than men, again at the zero-order level. In short, the existence of sex differences in work schedules represents one of the reasons why all the multivariate analyses in this report include a demographic control on type of worker.

5

Schedule Control and Other Factors Moderating the Effects of Work Schedules on Family Life

Analysis Strategy

Testing a Single Moderator Effect

In this section, we set forth the overall analysis strategy for detecting moderator effects. We refer back to the general discussion of analysis strategy in Chapter 3 and reiterate what was said about the basic test of a moderator effect. Given a set of demographic controls, a predictor, a moderator and a criterion, we construct a regression equation that includes the demographic controls, the predictor, the moderator, and the cross-product term formed by multiplying the predictor by the moderator. We then test whether the cross-product term makes a statistically significant incremental contribution to the variance accounted for in the criterion (Cohen, 1968).

Many — if not most — interactions, however, are more complicated than the basic case discussed in Chapter 3. One frequent complication is that predictors are measured by more than one term, for example, when a nominal (or categorical) predictor is represented by a series of dummy variables. In such cases, the regression equation includes terms representing the main effects of all the dummy variables except the one selected as a reference category; the equation, likewise, includes cross-product terms for each dummy variable except the reference category. The key statistical test becomes whether the *set* of cross-product terms jointly contribute significantly to the variance explained (Cohen, 1968).

A parallel (or additional) complication arises when the moderator variable is represented by more than one term. This can happen when the moderator is a nominal variable with three or more categories, in which case each category of the moderator is represented by a dummy variable and one category is designated as the reference. It can also happen when the conditioning effects of a continuously measured moderator are thought to be possibly nonlinear. The moderator is then divided into, e.g., three levels (high, medium and low) and is represented in terms of three dummy variables, one of which becomes the reference. Regardless of why the moderator is represented by several dummy variables, the regression equation includes all but one dummy variable as main effects and also all cross-product terms except one. As before, the test of the moderator effect is whether the cross-product terms jointly increment the variance explained.

Testing a Series of Moderator Effects

Actually, testing moderator effects is generally more involved than even the foregoing complexities suggest. Whereas our discussion thus far has concerned the testing of a single moderator effect, most research entails tests of a number of different moderator effects. Unfortunately, repeated use of the standard R^2 increment test allows Type I errors to mount steadily. As a consequence, we adopt an analytic strategy for handling multiple tests of conditioning effects that involves three separate components or steps: the protected t strategy, the counting strategy, and the criterion of substantive significance. In a sense, these three steps represent additional tests that any individually significant moderator effect must pass.

The protected t strategy.[1] The "protected t" strategy (Cohen and Cohen, 1975) is designed to keep the number of significance tests, and hence the number of Type I errors, to a minimum. The strategy takes advantage of the fact that just as one can perform a single test of the significance of a series of cross-product terms representing one predictor, one can also perform a single test of the incremental variance associated with a series of cross-product terms representing more than one predictor. For a single pairing of moderator and dependent variables, for example, one can test whether the cross-product terms based on all relevant predictors collectively make a significant contribution to explaining the variance of the dependent variable. The essence of the protected t strategy is to arrange one's significance tests hierarchically, starting at the highest or most general level and proceeding down the hierarchy if and only if initial tests prove significant; the strategy thus reduces the total number of tests performed.

For a particular combination of moderator and dependent variables, we would order the tests hierarchically as follows: (1) Taken as a set, do all the cross-product (or interaction) terms based on all the predictors significantly increase R^2? (2) If so, does the set of cross-product terms for one particular predictor increment R^2 significantly? (3) If so, and in cases in which either the predictor or moderator is represented by more than one term (e.g., by dummy variables) and where there is thus more than one cross-product term, does the cross-product term for a single component of the moderator and a single component of the predictor achieve significance? Only after all three questions have been answered affirmatively does a particular cross-product (i.e., interaction) term pass the protected t test. By allowing a test at one particular level of the hierarchy to substitute for multiple tests at the next level down, whenever possible, the foregoing strategy minimizes the number of tests and, thus, holds down the burgeoning rate of Type I errors.[2]

The counting strategy. Because the protected t strategy applies only to a particular pairing of moderator and dependent variables, we need a different approach to control Type I errors when several dependent variables are involved. Using the protected t strategy for a whole series of dependent variables, that is, will cause certain chance effects to be interpreted as significant. Hence, we invoke a second statistical strategy, termed the "counting" strategy. Specifically, we count the total number of significant effects obtained for a particular moderator and set of dependent variables (before the application of the protected t strategy), we compare this number against the total number of tests performed, and we then ask whether the number of significant results obtained could reasonably have occurred by chance alone. The counting strategy thus provides the broadest perspective (i.e., across predictors and across dependent variables) on whether chance levels have been exceeded. The strategy is not without its limitations, however. It produces no definitive conclusion as to whether a given array of significant effects may properly be attributed to chance, just a general impression as to whether a nonchance interpretation is justified. Furthermore, the strategy assumes that the various tests of significance are independent, an assumption that is technically incorrect although in practice it may prove to be a reasonable approximation.

The criterion of substantive significance. It is not sufficient, however, that moderator effects pass the tests contained in the protected t and counting strategies. Before we assign substantive significance to interactions, we further insist that the pattern of significant interactions be substantively meaningful and interpretable.

Schedule Control and Other Moderator Variables

As indicated earlier, a number of factors might condition the impact of work schedules on family life. The present analysis considers four moderator variables: schedule control plus the three demographic controls already discussed. The first moderator, *schedule control*, taps the degree to which a worker has a say as to what his or her work schedule will be. According to the fourth hypothesis enumerated in Chapter 2, schedule control moderates the negative relationships between nonstandard work schedules and the quality of family life; these negative relationships should be strongest when workers have least control over their work schedules.

The second candidate for moderator variable is the demographic variable that distinguishes the five *types of workers* defined in terms of sex, presence of spouse, and employment status of spouse. The impact of work schedules on family life might reasonably be thought greater for those types of workers who experience more life demands, yet have fewer general life resources. For example, work schedules might have more stringent family consequences for women than for men because of women's more extensive family responsibilities; likewise, there might be more consequences for those workers without a spouse than for those with one because a spouse offers resources for coping with job and family demands; there also might be more consequences for those with an employed spouse than for those with a nonemployed one because a spouse who works is less available to assist with one's own job and family demands.

Family life-cycle stage represents a third moderator variable. A reasonable conjecture here is that the impact of work schedules on family life will be greatest for parents of preschool children, somewhat less for parents of older children, and least for childless workers.

Education is the fourth and final conditioning variable. Our supposition is that work schedules will have their greatest effects on family life among the least educated workers because the latter group possesses the fewest life resources.

Measures of Schedule Control and Other Moderator Variables

Measurement of the four conditioning variables is also an important issue. The account that follows explains the measures of the moderator variables and, where relevant, provides basic distributional information. The index of schedule control is a mean of scores on three single-item ratings: "How hard do you think it would be to get the days you work changed permanently if you wanted them changed?" "How hard do you think it would be to get the hours you begin and end work changed permanently if you wanted them changed?" and "How hard is it for you to take time off during your workday to take care of personal or family matters?" In each case the response alternatives are: "Very hard," "somewhat hard," "not too hard," and "not at all hard."

Tables 5.1 through 5.4 set forth the distributions of responses to these three rating scales for the entire weighted analysis sample of individual workers and for men and women separately. For the first two items (ability to change days and hours), Tables 5.1 through 5.3 present joint bivariate distributions whose marginal frequencies represent univariate distributions; Table 5.4 displays the distributional data on the third item (time off work) on its own. Workers reportedly have only a limited capacity to change either the days or the hours they work. Fully two-thirds (67.3 percent) indicate that it would be very hard for them to change the days they work, and more than half (55.9 percent) report that it would be very difficult to get their hours changed. The table also points to an appreciable positive association between flexibility of days and hours; those workers who can change the days they work ("not at all hard") can generally also change their hours although the reverse does not hold as consistently. Workers experience much greater flexibility on the issue of getting time off work for personal matters. Almost three-quarters (73.9 percent) report that it is either not at all hard or not too hard to get some time off. Interestingly, 10 percent more men than women indicate that it is not at all hard to get time off, and this is the only sex difference that emerges for any of the univariate distributions on the three items on flexibility of schedule.

The internal reliability of the index of schedule control is only marginally satisfactory for this analysis of individual workers (alpha = .58). The two items about changing the days and hours one works intercorrelate substantially (r = .54) but these two items do not correlate strongly with the item about getting time off work for personal matters (r = .18 and r = .23, respectively).

Level of schedule control provides us with a choice between two modes of measurement: dummy variables and a continuous measure. For the dummy variable version, we trichotomize schedule control (high, medium, low) and convert the three levels to dummy variables, one of which (low control) is omitted from the regression and treated as the reference category. For example, in the simplest interaction involving only one predictor measured by one term, $2 \times 1 = 2$ cross-product terms would be entered into the regression equation; two predictors, each measured by one term, would require $2 \times 2 = 4$ cross-product

TABLE 5.1
Ease of Changing Hours by Ease of Changing Days:
All Workers[a]

Ease of Changing Hours	Ease of Changing Days				
	Not at All Hard to Change Days	Not Too Hard	Somewhat Hard	Very Hard	All Levels
Not at All Hard to Change Hours	105 64.8%	30 15.6%	2 1.2%	63 5.8%	200 12.4%
Not Too Hard	22 13.6	80 41.7	37 21.4	106 9.8	245 15.2
Somewhat Hard	14 8.6	39 20.3	77 44.5	135 12.5	265 16.4
Very Hard	21 13.0	43 22.4	57 32.9	780 72.0	901 55.9
All Levels[b]	162 10.1	192 11.9	173 10.7	1084 67.3	1611 100

[a]Weighted distribution.
[b]Percents add up to 100 across this row; all others are column percents.

TABLE 5.2
Ease of Changing Hours by Ease of Changing Days:
Men Only[a]

Ease of Changing Hours	Ease of Changing Days				
	Not at All Hard to Change Days	Not Too Hard	Somewhat Hard	Very Hard	All Levels
Not at All Hard to Change Hours	64 60.4%	22 18.0%	2 2.1%	46 6.7%	134 13.3%
Not Too Hard	20 18.9	45 36.9	16 16.7	60 8.8	141 14.0
Somewhat Hard	7 6.6	24 19.7	41 42.7	83 12.2	155 15.4
Very Hard	15 14.2	31 25.4	37 38.5	494 72.3	577 57.3
All Levels[b]	106 10.5	122 12.1	96 9.5	683 67.8	1007 100

[a]Weighted distribution.
[b]Percents add up to 100 across this row; all others are column percents.

TABLE 5.3

Ease of Changing Hours by Ease of Changing Days:
Women Only[a]

Ease of Changing Hours	Ease of Changing Days				
	Not at All Hard to Change Days	Not Too Hard	Somewhat Hard	Very Hard	All Levels
Not at All Hard to Change Hours	41 73.2%	8 11.4%	0 0.0%	17 4.2%	66 10.9%
Not Too Hard	2 3.6	35 50.0	21 27.3	46 11.5	104 17.2
Somewhat Hard	7 12.5	15 21.4	36 46.8	52 13.0	110 18.2
Very Hard	6 10.7	12 17.1	20 26.0	286 71.3	324 53.6
All Levels[b]	56 9.3	70 11.6	77 12.7	401 66.4	604 100

[a]Weighted distribution.
[b]Percents add up to 100 across this row; all others are column percents.

TABLE 5.4

Ease of Getting Time off Work
for Personal Matters by Sex[a]

Ease of Getting Time off Work	Worker's Sex		All Workers
	Men	Women	
Not at All Hard to Take Time off Work	426 42.8%	194 32.8%	620 39.1%
Not Too Hard	337 33.8	215 36.4	552 34.8
Somewhat Hard	107 10.7	71 12.0	178 11.2
Very Hard	126 12.7	111 18.8	237 14.9
All levels[b]	996 62.8	591 37.2	1587 100

[a]Weighted distribution.
[b]Percents add up to 100 across this row; all others are column percents.

terms, and so on. For the continuous measure of schedule control, by comparison, the number of cross-product terms would equal the number of predictor terms.

Our strategy is first to use the dummy variable measures and, thereby, to determine whether most conditioning effects of schedule control involve a monotonic increase or decrease in the slope of the conditioned relationship. If so, we can then use the continuous measure of schedule control to create the interaction terms. The latter method provides a somewhat more restrictive interaction test (i.e., linear only) but one that is statistically more powerful. A significant interaction test based on the continuous measure of schedule control would indicate that the slope of the regression of a measure of family life on a work schedule characteristic increases or decreases a constant number of units for each unit increase in schedule control.

The next three moderator variables are the previously discussed demographic controls. To recapitulate, five dummy variables correspond to the five types of workers but one of the five (sole breadwinning husbands) is omitted from the regression and becomes the reference category. Similarly, the five categories of family life-cycle stage are represented by five dummy variables, one of which (childless workers forty-five or over) converts to the reference category. Like schedule control, education provides us with two alternatives: a dummy variable version based on four levels of education (less than high school diploma, high school diploma, some college, college degree and above), the first of which becomes the reference category; and a continuous measure (actually eight levels). Again, we analyze moderator effects based on the dummy variable measures before we use the continuous form.

Main Effects of Schedule Control

Although schedule control functions primarily as a moderator variable in the current analyses, its main effects on measures of family life remain of interest. To examine its effects under multivariate control, we consider the regressions that include as predictors the demographic controls, the various work schedule characteristics, and the two dummy variables measuring schedule control.

According to the regression data (not shown in a table), schedule control has significant main effects on only two of the six measures of family life: total work/family conflict and hours conflict. In each case, the main effects are monotonically decreasing across the three levels of schedule control, meaning that conflict is highest for low control, intermediate for medium control, and lowest for high control. Again, for each case, the difference in conflict between low and high control achieves statistical significance (b = −.254 and −.110 for total conflict and hours conflict, respectively) but the comparison between low and medium control does not.

Overall Results for Moderator Effects of Schedule Control and Other Variables

As noted, in order to be regarded as interpretable, moderator effects based on the three work schedule characteristics should pass several tests. Individually, they should satisfy the standard R^2 increment test. For the relevant pairing of moderator and dependent variables, they should also pass the (remaining) tests that make up the protected t strategy. For the relevant moderator, they should likewise survive the tests of the counting strategy when the latter is applied to all six dependent variables collectively. Finally, the pattern of statistically significant conditioning effects should prove to be substantively meaningful.

The counting strategy allows us to compare the four moderator variables in terms of the number of significant conditioning effects they generate based on all three predictors and all six dependent variables. The counting strategy thus permits us to compare the set of significant interactions obtained for each moderator against chance as well as against the other moderators. The maximum number of significant interactions for each moderator is 18 (3 predictors × 6 dependent variables). According to the counting strategy, on a chance basis alone we would expect approximately one significant conditioning effect at $p < .05$ (.05 × 18 = 1 approx.) and two significant effects at $p < .10$ (.10 × 18 = 2 approx.) for each moderator; in short, the most likely outcome would be one significant conditioning effect at $p < .05$ and, in addition, one at $p < .10$.

As explained earlier, schedule control may be assessed by either dummy variable or continuous measures. We report the data for the dummy variable measure of schedule control because, unlike the main effects of this measure (all of which were shown to be monotonic), not all of its conditioning effects involve a monotonic increase (or decrease) in the slope of the conditioned relationships. That is, the continuous measure does not capture all of the theoretically meaningful conditioning effects of schedule control and does not detect all of the effects detected using dummy variables. The data based on the dummy variable measure of schedule control pass the various tests of the protected t strategy and generate one significant moderator effect at $p < .05$ and three additional ones at $p < .10$. In other words, there are four cases where an interaction between schedule control and a predictor is significant at $p < .10$ for one of the dependent variables and where, in addition, the interactions between schedule control and the full set of predictors make a significant contribution (at $p < .10$ or better) to the variance of the dependent variable. These are the four conditioning effects that survive the protected t strategy. Moreover, because these four moderator effects obtained at $p < .10$ surpass the two expected by chance, the data on conditioning effects involving schedule control are above chance levels as defined by the counting strategy; in short, they pass the test of the counting strategy as well.

The results for the demographic variable that distinguishes the five types of workers are four significant moderator effects at $p < .05$ that survive the protected t strategy; for family life-cycle stage the comparable results are similar, three at $p < .05$. For these two demographic variables, then, the numbers of significant interactions obtained are in excess of what would be expected by chance as defined by the counting strategy. In the case of education, we may again consider the results for both types of measures, dummy variable and continuous. Neither measure of education, however, generates enough significant interactions to surpass by a nontrivial margin the number expected purely on the basis of chance as defined by the counting strategy. In consequence, the analysis of the moderator effects of education proceeds no further.

Ironically, of the three moderators that pass all tests required by the protected t and counting strategies (i.e., schedule control plus the first two demographic variables), only schedule control, the one that performs the least well statistically, generates an interpretable pattern of findings. In short, only schedule control produces a pattern of significant conditioning effects which are both clearly more numerous than might be expected by chance and substantively and theoretically interpretable. As a consequence, the data on type of worker and family life-cycle stage as moderators are consigned to Appendix B, which includes both a tabular display and a brief textual summary.

Moderator Effects of Schedule Control

For the detailed analysis of the moderator effects of schedule control, we switch to a more precise language for describing conditioning effects. The technique adopted for gaining greater analytic precision is to count the number of significant effects differently from the way used to compare results for the four different moderators. Whenever a predictor or moderator variable is measured by more than one term in a regression equation (e.g., by dummy variable terms), we count the number of separate terms rather than the number of original variables. Accordingly, it requires seven terms to represent the three predictor variables (two terms for pattern of days worked, four for shiftwork, and one for number of hours worked each week) and two terms to represent the dummy variable version of the moderator, schedule control. Counted this way, the maximum possible number of conditioning effects for schedule control far exceeds the earlier figure (eighteen). To take a hypothetical example, instead of discussing the interaction between schedule control and shiftwork with total work/family conflict as the dependent variable, we might now concentrate on the interaction between one of the components of schedule control (e.g., high control) and one of the components of shiftwork (e.g., afternoon shift), retaining the same dependent variable. It may be noted parenthetically that this shift from an analysis based on original variables to one based on individual regression terms represents a shift from a higher to a lower level of aggregation within the protected t strategy.

The data based on schedule control as moderator and work schedule characteristics as predictors appear in Tables 5.5 and 5.6. Table 5.5 indicates which relationships between measures of work schedules and family life are moderated significantly by schedule control and whether such significant moderator effects are in the expected direction. Table 5.6 provides basic statistical information on the significant moderator effects. Entries in the first three columns of Table 5.6 are estimated metric coefficients within each level of schedule control net of other variables; these regression coefficients express changes in the dependent variable (family life) which would result from a change of one unit in the independent variable (work schedule characteristic). The fourth column presents the main effect of the work schedule characteristic (across all levels of schedule control). In the case of one work schedule characteristic (number of hours worked), it actually presents the main effect of the linear component of the characteristic with the data taken from an equation that also includes a main effect for the quadratic component of the characteristic. The last two columns of Table 5.6 document the strength of the various conditioning effects as measured by the amount of incremental variance that each effect accounts for.

Although we do not find a large number of significant moderator effects based on schedule control, we do find some important ones. According to the results in Tables 5.5 and 5.6, only six of the possible moderator effects prove to be significant. Of these six, five are in the

TABLE 5.5
Summary of Moderator Effects of Schedule Control on the Relationships between Work Schedule Characteristics and Family Measures

Work Schedule Characteristics (Indep. Var.)	Family Measures (Dep. Var.)					
	Time in Child Care	Time in Housework	Total Conflict	Hours Conflict	Schedule Conflict	Family Adjustment
Nonvariable Weekend Days					Predicted effect #5 (under high sched. control, weekend work slightly decreases schedule conflict)	
Variable Days						
Afternoon Shift	Predicted effects #1 and #2 (under med. and high sched. control, aft. shift increases child care time)					
Night Shift	Predicted effect #3 (under high sched. control, night shift increases child care time substantially)					
Rotating Shift						
Other Shift						
Number of Hours				Predicted effect #4 (under high sched. control, positive effect of number of hours worked on hours conflict is weaker)		Opposite of predicted effect (under high sched. control, number of hours worked increases schedule conflict)

TABLE 5.6

Conditioning Effects of Schedule Control on Relationships between Work
Schedule Characteristics and Family Measures

Family Measures (Dep. Var.) Work Schedule Characteristics (Indep. Var.)	Effect of Work Schedule Characteristic When Schedule Control Is:[a]			Main Effect	Increment to R^2 Due to Interaction[b]	
	Low	Med.	High		Med.	High
Time in Child Care						
Afternoon Shift	− 3.427	7.843*	13.296**	3.522	.0086	
Night Shift	1.063	.607	15.245*	3.296	−	.0047
Hours Conflict						
Number of Hours Worked	.0168	.0132	.0090*	.0095	−	.0042
Schedule Conflict						
Nonvariable Weekend Days	.119	.211	− .013+	.082*	−	.0026
Number of HOurs Worked	− .00258	.00007	.00384*	.00418	−	.0048

+p<.10.
*p<.05.
**p<.01.
[a]Significance levels of regression coefficients for interaction refer to comparisons between the category indicated and the referent category (low schedule control).
[b]Increments to R^2 for significant interactions refer to comparisons between regression coefficients for the category indicated and the referent category (low schedule control).

direction predicted by the fourth hypothesis. In these five cases, that is, departures from a standard work schedule do not have the degree of negative impact under conditions of medium or high schedule control that they do under conditions of low schedule control. In fact, for three of the five moderator effects in the expected direction, the effect of the work schedule characteristic changes sign under conditions of medium or high schedule control, meaning that in these three cases the effect of a nonstandard work schedule on family life is actually *positive* (as opposed to being merely less negative) under conditions of medium or high schedule control. Among dependent variables, child-care time generates the most effects in the predicted direction (three), followed by hours conflict and schedule conflict (one effect each). Among predictors, shiftwork generates the largest number of expected effects (three) followed by number of hours worked and pattern of days worked (one each).

Having talked in aggregate terms about the five conditioning effects in the predicted direction, we may now consider them one at a time. According to the first two conditioning effects in Tables 5.5 and 5.6, schedule control moderates the relationship between afternoon shift and time spent with one's children. Whereas working an afternoon (as opposed to a day) shift decreases the amount of time one spends with one's children by over three hours a week under low schedule control, working an afternoon shift increases parental time by almost eight hours per week under medium schedule control (moderator effect #1 in the tables) and under high schedule control the increase is more than thirteen hours per week (moderator effect #2). Thus, in the case of afternoon shift and child-care time, the moderator effects of schedule control are clearly monotonic; as schedule control moves from low to medium to high, the effect of afternoon shift on child-care time becomes increasingly favorable.

Schedule control also moderates the effect of night shift on child-care time. Under conditions of low schedule control, working a night (as opposed to a day) shift increases parental time by just one hour per week; yet, working a night shift increases parental time by fifteen hours a week under high schedule control (moderator effect #3). The conditioning effect is not monotonic, however, because the positive effect of night shift on time with children does not consistently increase as schedule control increases. Instead, the (positive) effect of night shift on parental time is about the same for low and medium schedule control (i.e., approximately one hour). The relevant regression coefficients in Table 5.6 make clear that this third conditioning effect includes no sign change.

Next is the interaction involving number of hours worked and hours conflict. The positive impact of number of hours worked on reports of hours conflict is greater under low than high schedule control (moderator effect #4). The interaction follows a monotonic pattern; the impact of hours worked on conflict decreases as schedule control increases but only the comparison between low and high schedule control achieves statistical significance. Again the conditioning effect entails no change of sign.

The fifth interaction in the predicted direction introduces the pattern of days worked as the independent variable. Working regularly on weekends (as opposed to regular work on weekdays only) increases schedule conflict under conditions of low schedule control but decreases such conflict under high schedule control. The regression coefficients for the three levels of schedule control do not display a monotonic pattern; in fact, the effect of weekend work on schedule conflict is more positive for medium than for low schedule control but not significantly so.

These five moderator effects in the expected direction call for additional interpretation and explanation. We focus here on two issues, the pattern of sign changes in the moderator effects of schedule control and the causal mechanisms by which schedule control acts as a moderator. In the first instance, the observed pattern of sign changes makes good sense. Nonstandard work shifts on a typical day (and, to a much smaller extent, nonstandard days worked in a typical week) may have positive effects on family life when work schedules are substantially under the control of the worker, even though their effects may be negative under conditions of low schedule control. (These are cases of moderator effects *with* sign changes.) By contrast, the number of hours worked in a typical week should never have a positive effect on the amount of time spent in family roles, or a negative effect on work/family conflict; at best, high schedule control should ameliorate (but not reverse) the negative effects of the number of hours worked on the various measures of family life. (These are cases of conditioning effects *without* sign changes.) We will return shortly to the issue of sign changes in moderator effects when attempting to explain the one finding in the unexpected direction.

By what specific mechanisms, we may next ask, does schedule control moderate the effects of work schedules on family life? This question calls attention to the three component measures of the index of schedule control: control over days worked, control over hours worked, and ability to get limited time off work for personal business. If we view the index as measuring control over *when* the person works, as all three items would to some degree suggest, it is highly plausible that schedule control can diminish the harmful effects of *amount* of time worked by scheduling work at convenient times. Such reasoning would apply to the fourth moderator effect in the tables. Also plausible is the argument that control over *when* one works can mitigate the (usually harmful) effects of nonstandard work schedules. Even if one must regularly work on weekends, for example, control over exactly which weekend pattern one works may still be beneficial. The notion here is simply that micro-adjustments can diminish the impact of macro-arrangements. This second argument applies to interactions 1, 2, 3, and 5 in Table 5.5. In addition, if schedule control also refers to control over *how much time* is spent working, as the item on getting time off work suggests, it may moderate the effects of nonstandard schedules by diminishing the amount of time they require. Again, the relevant moderator effects are 1, 2, 3, and 5. Needless to say, the foregoing alternative interpretations of the index of schedule control need not be regarded as mutually exclusive; in fact, all may be simultaneously operative to varying degrees.

It remains only to report and discuss the one moderator effect in the unexpected direction, namely, the finding that number of hours worked is positively related to reports of schedule conflict under high schedule control but negatively related under low control (moderator effect #6). The explanation offered here begins with the fact that schedule conflict (the dependent variable) and hours conflict are alternative responses to an open-ended question about the nature of work/family conflict, and are thus negatively (though artifactually) related among individuals reporting work/family conflict ($r = -.23$). As a result, the interaction involving number of hours worked and hours conflict, an interaction that is both expected and observed, is matched by an artifactual interaction in the unexpected direction involving number of hours worked and schedule conflict. Two factors underscore the artifactual nature of the unexpected moderator effect: the observed negative relationship between reports of hours conflict and schedule conflict among workers reporting work/family conflict; and the fact that the conditioning effect includes a sign change when conditioning effects involving number of hours worked should not and otherwise do not include sign changes.

Summary

This chapter examines interactions between four moderator variables (schedule control and three demographic controls) and three work schedule characteristics (pattern of days worked, shift, and number of hours worked per week), with family measures as the dependent variables. To minimize Type I errors, the analysis adopts a highly conservative approach to the testing of moderator effects. Specifically, it requires that all potential moderator effects pass the tests of the protected t strategy, the counting strategy, and the criterion of substantive significance. Three of the moderators (schedule control, type of worker, and family life-cycle stage) survive the protected t and counting strategies but only one (schedule control) also meets the criterion of substantive significance. Actually, schedule control generates four conditioning effects that pass all relevant tests but we divide the four significant conditioning effects into their six significant components and report instead on the six components.

Five of these six components involving schedule control represent interactions in the direction predicted by the fourth hypothesis enumerated in Chapter 2. In each of the five cases, that is, departures from a standard work schedule have a less negative (or more positive) impact under conditions of medium or high schedule control than they do under low schedule control. The five cases are as follows. First, whereas working an afternoon shift decreases time spent with children by over three hours per week under low schedule control, working an afternoon shift increases parental time by almost eight hours per week under medium schedule control. Second, the corresponding increase under high schedule control is more than thirteen hours per week. Third, under conditions of low schedule control, working a night shift increases time in child care by only one hour per week but working a night shift increases parental time by fifteen hours per week under high schedule control. Fourth, the positive effect of number of hours worked per week on hours conflict is greater under low schedule control than high schedule control. Fifth and finally, regular weekend work increases schedule conflict under low schedule control, yet decreases such conflict under high schedule control. Here, then, are five distinct examples of how schedule control, functioning as a moderator variable, improves the effects of nonstandard work schedules on family life.

Notes

1. Since our analysis makes use of House's account of regression methodology (House, 1980), it seems worth pointing out certain technical differences between the regression procedures used here for testing moderator effects and those used by House. In the first place, we adopt the protected t strategy and House does not. This means that we test for interaction hierarchically: first, interactions involving all predictors, then interactions involving single predictors, then interactions involving components of predictors. House confines his significance testing to the second level of the hierarchy, namely, interactions involving single predictors. A second difference is that we follow a "step-down" approach to significance testing whereas House uses a "step-up" approach. That is, to test for a particular moderator effect, we determine the *loss* of explained variance when an interaction is omitted from an equation containing all interaction terms; House assesses the *gain* in explained variance when an interaction is added to an equation containing no interaction terms. In other words, we test the statistical contribution of an interaction, controlling for all other interaction terms; House tests for an interaction in the absence of any other interactions. Our procedure is thus more conservative than his in that it accepts as significant only those interactions that have been demonstrated to exist independently of other (possibly confounded) interactions.

2. For the F tests of various moderator effects (i.e., single moderator effects, protected t strategy), our analysis includes $p < .10$ along with $p < .05$ and $p < .01$ as acceptable levels of statistical significance. The addition of $p < .10$ to the two conventional levels of significance ($p < .05$, $p < .01$) requires some justification. Based as they are on the general linear model, the moderated regression procedures used here for detecting interactions are distinctly conservative; that is, in standard R^2 increment tests, they automatically assign any overlapping variance between additive (i.e., main) and nonadditive (i.e., interactive) effects to the additive column. Because the regression procedures make it difficult to find significant moderator effects, less stringent levels of significance can help offset this conservative bias.

6

Dual-Earner Couples: Patterns of Joint Schedules and Effects on Family Life

Introduction

The growing number of dual-earner couples (Hayghe, 1981) in our economy prompts particular interest in the impact of dual work schedules on family life. Previous chapters and Appendix B include comparisons of husbands and wives in two-earner families with sole breadwinning husbands, sole breadwinning wives, and female single parents. These analyses suggest that dual-earner husbands perform somewhat more housework and child care than do their sole breadwinning counterparts, though still considerably less than dual-earner wives. Dual-earner husbands do not differ from sole breadwinning husbands in total work/family conflict or any of its components; however, they appear to have less conflict, especially concerning scheduling, than dual-earner wives. Further, dual-earner husbands differ little from sole breadwinners in family adjustment; the former register more positive family adjustment than dual-earner wives, though the precise form of the statistical comparison in the earlier analysis does not indicate whether the difference is significant.

Further, our previous analyses indicate that the number of hours worked appears to have a more negative impact on time in child care among dual-earner wives than among dual-earner husbands. In two-earner couples, both the night shift and rotating shift seem to have stronger effects in elevating total work/family conflict among husbands than wives; the residual category of "other" shifts, however, increases total conflict more among wives than husbands. The statistical strategy used in the earlier analyses, however, required comparing dual-earner husbands and wives (as well as female single parents and sole bread-winning wives) only to sole breadwinning husbands and not to each other.

These findings do not exhaust the analyses of husbands and wives in two-earner families made possible by the 1977 Quality of Employment Survey. Since married respondents were asked to describe their spouses' job schedules in addition to their own, we can analyze five general questions about two-earner couples, several of which have been largely unexplored in past research. Each is introduced below and then considered in detail.

1. *How do husbands' and wives' job schedules compare in the aggregate, and how are their schedules related to each other at the within-couple level?* Previous studies provide limited information on a variety of fundamental descriptive points concerning two-earner couples. Evidence that men generally work longer hours than women (Quinn and Staines, 1979) might suggest that the same holds true in two-earner couples, though previous studies rarely make this comparison. Our analyses in Chapter 3 indicate that men are more likely than women to have schedules including regular weekend work, but, perhaps surprisingly, are no more likely to have nondaytime shiftwork. We shall see whether the same patterns appear in two-earner couples.

Within couples, spouses' schedules may be similar, complementary, or unrelated. Duncan and Hill (1975) and Lein et al. (1974), for example, have described the "different shift" pattern, in which one spouse works during the day and the other works a nonday shift, presumably to reduce the need for child care arrangements. This pattern suggests that spouses' schedules are complementary in terms of shift in at least some couples. Earlier research did not address the question of similarity vs. complementarity in other schedule characteristics in dual-earner couples.

2. *What are the most prevalent joint patterns of husbands' and wives' job schedules, and how do these patterns vary by family life-cycle stage and other variables?* The distributions of and relationships between husbands' and wives' schedules determine the prevalence of the various possible joint patterns of schedules. Duncan and Hill (1975) note that the different shift pattern is evident in about 16 percent of the dual-earner parents of young children in the Panel Study of Income Dynamics. Lein et al. (1974) also observed this pattern in about half of a much smaller sample of two-earner families with preschool children. In our data, the prevalence of this and other patterns involving other schedule characteristics can be examined, as can the relationship be-

tween these patterns and background variables. For example, both Duncan and Hill (1975) and Lein et al. (1974) implicitly suggest that the different shift pattern occurs most frequently in dual-earner families with young children. However, these studies did not formally test that hypothesis.

3. *How does an individual's schedule affect his or her family life, and how do these effects vary by sex?* As indicated in Chapter 2, many previous studies examined schedule/family relationships only in males. As noted, however, Robinson's (1977) data suggest that time in paid work has a stronger inverse relationship to housework time in husbands than in wives. Keith and Schafer (1980) find that number of work hours predicts work/family conflict better among husbands than wives, but they do not test this difference for significance. Previous studies provide few other data on sex differences in schedule/family relationships.

4. *What "cross-over" effects does the spouse's schedule have on an individual's family life, and how do these effects vary by sex?* In addition to the effects of an individual's schedule on his or her own family life, there may also be "cross-over" effects, where an individual's family behavior is affected by the spouse's schedule. For example, a husband who has a "normal" schedule, and who therefore is expected to show average levels of housework, child care, work/family conflict, and the like, may nonetheless show distinctive alterations in his behavior due to features of his spouse's schedule. Studies discussed in Chapter 2 (Walker and Woods, 1976; Meissner et al., 1975; Greenhaus and Kopelman, 1981; Keith and Schafer, 1980) provide evidence both for and against such cross-over effects in two-earner couples. Walker and Woods (1976) found that a husband's number of paid work hours was positively associated with his wife's time in housework, but a wife's paid worktime bore no relationship to her husband's housework. Keith and Schafer (1980) find that a husband's work time predicts his wife's work/family conflict, but a wife's worktime does not predict her husband's conflict. Greenhaus and Kopelman (1981) observe no relationship, however, between a wife's work hours and her husband's conflict.

5. *How do the schedules of an individual and his or her spouse interact to influence the individual's family life, and do these interactions vary for husbands and wives?* This topic has not been investigated in earlier research. For example, regular shiftwork outside of the usual daytime hours for either an individual or a spouse may ordinarily increase the individual's work/family conflict, but when both spouses have shiftwork, conflict may be particularly intensified. The possible effects of such patterns, as well as differences in these patterns, can be investigated by examining interactions between spouses' schedules.

Methodology

Sample

The sample used in these analyses is the 274 dual-earner husbands and 226 dual-earner wives in the 1977 Quality of Employment Survey, drawn from the larger analysis sample used in earlier chapters. These respondents provided information about their own work schedules, their spouses' work schedules, and their own family lives. Although the sample includes 274 husbands and 226 wives, it provides information about the schedules of 500 husbands and 500 wives. It is thus considered a sample of 500 two-earner couples, with the husband the informant in some cases and the wife in others. In effect, this analysis uses fewer cases but has more information for each case than the analysis reported in earlier chapters.

It must be noted that a less stringent criterion was used to classify a primary respondent's spouse as employed than was used to select the primary respondent. To be eligible for the survey, primary respondents had to be employed twenty or more hours per week. For a primary respondent to be classified as a dual-earner husband or wife, however, no minimum number of hours was required for the spouse, as long as he or she was reported to be working for pay. Thus, technically, the sample includes two subgroups, one group representative of dual-career couples in which the husband works at least twenty hours per week and the other group representative of two-earner couples in which the wife works at least twenty hours per week.

The sample is not weighted for analyses of either distributions or relationships. It should be recalled that the sample weight is the number of persons in the household currently employed twenty or more hours a week. Almost all the two-earner couples had sample weights of two. A few had weights of one because the spouse was employed less than twenty hours per week; a few had weights of three or more because of additional earners. Differences between weighted and unweighted distributions are thus extremely small.

Demographic Controls

This chapter employs two demographic control variables in addition to those used in earlier analyses. The presence or absence of formal child care arrangements is used as a control variable. In the survey, dual-earner husbands and wives with children twelve or under in their household were asked whether their children were regularly cared for by any of three different kinds of formal child care arrangements while they were at work: group care, family care (care in another person's home), or home care (care by a relative or nonrelative in one's own home). About 50 percent of both dual-earner husbands and wives reported using at least one of these arrangements (see Pleck et al., 1980). This variable was included in analyses in this chapter because of its potential impact on couples' schedule patterns as well as on the dependent variables.

The Duncan Socioeconomic Index was also used as a control variable. This variable is coded from the respondent's occupation and in crosstabulational analyses is collapsed into a white collar/blue collar dichotomy. The items providing the basis for these additional control variables are included in Appendix A.

Predictor Variables (Work Schedule Characteristics)

Because this analysis focuses on schedule patterns of couples, the schedule variables used here differ somewhat from those used in earlier chapters in which the individual was the unit of analysis. Specifically, the shift variable used earlier is simplified by collapsing it into fewer categories, and certain other schedule variables, available for both respondent and spouse in the survey, are introduced. The primary variables used here for both individuals and their spouses are:

1. Pattern of days worked, classified as:
   Regular, nonweekend days only
   Regular, includes a weekend day
   Variable days
2. Shift (defined according to starting time), classified as:
   Early day shift, 3:30-7:59 a.m. starting time (about 75 percent of these occur between 7:00 and 7:59 a.m.)
   Late day shift, 8:00-11:59 a.m. starting time (about 75 percent of these occur between 8:00 and 8:59 a.m.)
   Nonday shift, all other regular starting times
   Variable, not the same starting time each day
3. Number of hours worked per week
4. Number of days worked per week (for those working a regular number of days)
5. Second job (present or absent)
6. Ending time, classified as:
   12:01 a.m.-2:59 p.m.
   3:00-3:59 p.m.
   4:00-4:59 p.m.
   5:00-5:59 p.m.

6:00 p.m.-midnight
Variable, not the same ending time each day

The shift categories (in variable 2 above) differ somewhat from those used earlier. The construction of pattern variables and the examination of interaction effects involving the schedules of both individuals and their spouses make the consolidation of low frequency categories desirable. Thus, afternoon and night are combined into nonday shift; rotating and other are grouped as variable. The day shift is disaggregated into early and late categories for crosstabulational analyses. In regression analyses, they are combined as a single category.

The items providing the basis for the schedule variables not used earlier are included in Appendix A.

Analysis Strategy

Analysis of the first two questions concerning the distributions and patterns of spouses' schedules employs crosstabulations — first of husbands' by wives' schedules and then of pattern variables combining husbands' and wives' schedules by demographic variables.

Analysis of the remaining questions raises several issues of statistical strategy and presentation. One basic constraint in the research design is that while respondents report both their own and their spouses' schedules, they report family outcome variables only for themselves. Thus, the effects of the spouse's schedule on the individual can be examined but the two possible pathways for these effects cannot be distinguished. These pathways are the direct effect of, for example, a wife's schedule on her husband's family life and the indirect effect of a wife's schedule on her husband via the effects of her schedule on her family life, which then affects his family life. Ideally, while these two pathways should be differentiated, the present design only permits estimates of their sum without distinguishing them from one another.

It should be emphasized, however, that the present design does permit controlling for another kind of indirect cross-over effect. There may be systematic associations between features of husbands' and wives' schedules. If so, the effects of a spouse's and an individual's schedules on the individual's family life will be confounded. As a result, the wife's work schedule, for instance, may appear to affect the husband's family life only because her schedule is associated with characteristics of his schedule which have distinctive impacts on his family life. For example, as noted earlier, some research suggests that two-earner husbands and wives with small children may seek to work different shifts. In such couples, having a spouse working a daytime shift may appear to have a negative impact on the individual's family life because the latter is more likely to work a nonday shift. In our data, the effect of the spouse's schedule on the individual's family life can be examined, controlling for this kind of confounding effect.

Regression results concerning the impacts of schedules on family life are presented separately for each sex. For main effects of the individual's and the spouse's schedules on the individual's family life, sex differences in coefficients are tested for significance using the regression procedure for evaluating conditioning effects presented earlier. Interactions between individuals' and spouses' schedules are tested for each sex using the same method.

Distributions of and Relationships between Spouses' Schedules

Pattern of Days Worked

Table 6.1 crosstabulates two-earner husbands' and wives' pattern of days worked. This and later tables in this format permit comparison of husbands' and wives' distributions on work schedule characteristics in the aggregate (by comparison of row and column marginals) and examination of the relationship between husbands' and wives' schedule characteristics at the within-couple level.

Earlier analyses (Tables 3.5 and 3.6) suggested that, in the full sample, men were more likely than women to work on weekends. Our analysis within the more restricted sample of two-earner couples also indicates that two-earner husbands and wives have significantly different distributions in their pattern of days worked. The marginals in Table 6.1 indicate that the major difference is that husbands, more often than wives, work at least one weekend day on a regular basis: 24.4 percent vs. 15.6 percent. Husbands have regular weekday and variable schedules somewhat less often than do wives.

Husbands' and wives' patterns of days are significantly associated with each other in two-earner couples. These patterns are more similar than would be expected by chance: a husband or wife who works a regular weekday schedule is more likely to have a spouse with the same kind of schedule; a husband or wife with a schedule involving weekend work on a regular basis is more likely to have a spouse with the same; and likewise for working a variable schedule.

TABLE 6.1

Wife's Pattern of Days Worked
by Husband's Pattern of Days Worked[a]

| Wife's Pattern of Days Worked | Husband's Pattern of Days Worked | | | All Patterns |
	Regular, Nonweekend	Regular, Weekend	Variable	
Regular, Nonweekend	225	74	37	336
	71.0%	60.7%	60.7%	67.2%
Regular, Weekend	42	28	8	78
	13.2	23.0	13.1	15.6
Variable	50	20	16	86
	15.8	16.4	26.2	17.2
All Patterns[b]	317	122	61	500
	63.5	24.4	12.2	

[a]Difference between husband's and wife's distributions (comparison of row and column marginals): $X^2 = 14.48$, 2 df, $p < .001$; association between husband's and wife's pattern of days work: $X^2 = 10.75$, 4 df, $p < .05$.
[b]Percents add up to 100 across this row; all other percents are column percents.

Shift

Earlier results in the full analysis sample (Tables 3.5 and 3.6) suggested no sex difference in the distribution of shift worked; women are just as likely as men to work day, afternoon, night or rotating shifts.

Using somewhat different categories, Table 6.2 compares dual-earner husbands' and wives' shifts. The proportions of dual-earner husbands and wives in nonday shifts (7.5 vs. 9.6 percent) and in variable shifts (18.7 vs. 18.9 percent) are similar and consistent with the earlier analysis. However, the proportions differ markedly in two shift categories not distinguished in the previous analysis: dual-earner husbands work an early day shift far more often and work late day shifts far less often than do dual-earner wives. The differences in frequencies in these two shift categories are large enough to make husbands' and wives' overall distributions significantly different.

Husbands' and wives' shifts show no statistically significant relationship to each other. That is, a husband working on one particular shift schedule is neither more nor less likely to have a wife who is working any other particular schedule. Husbands and wives may attempt to select job shifts in accommodation to each other, but it appears either that they have relatively little freedom to do so or that one spouse may accommodate to the same schedule in the other in a variety of different

TABLE 6.2
Wife's Shift by Husband's Shift[a]

| Wife's Shift | Husband's Shift | | | | All Shifts |
	Early Day Shift	Late Day Shift	Nonday Shift	Variable	
Early Day Shift (3:30–7:59 a.m. starting time)	58	32	7	22	119
	28.3%	20.3%	18.9%	23.4%	24.2%
Late Day Shift (8:00–11:59 a.m. starting time)	89	88	17	39	233
	43.4	55.7	45.9	42.4	47.4
Nonday Shift	25	11	5	8	47
	12.2	6.7	13.5	8.7	9.6
Variable	35	27	8	23	93
	17.1	17.1	27.6	25.0	18.9
All Shifts[b]	205	158	37	92	492
	41.7	32.1	7.5	18.7	100

[a]Difference between husband's and wife's distributions (comparison of row and column marginals): $X^2 = 38.46$, 3df, $p < .001$; association between husband's and wife's shift: $X^2 = 11.82$, 9 df, ns.
[b]Percents add up to 100 across this row; all other percents are column percents.

ways. Thus, while earlier analysis showed that, at the within-couple level, husbands' and wives' patterns of days worked each week tend to be similar, their patterns of hours worked each day appear to be unrelated.

Table C.1 in Appendix C gives a more detailed crosstabulation of spouses' starting times, and Table C.2 provides a crosstabulation of spouses' ending times. The latter indicates that husbands have later ending times significantly more often. Thus, on the average, husbands both start work earlier and end work later than wives.

Amount of Time Worked: Number of Hours and Days Per Week

Tables 6.3 and 6.4 display two-earner couples' patterns of the amount of time worked, as indicated both by the number of hours per week and the number of days per week. In view of the large proportions (one-third) of both husbands and wives reporting they work exactly forty hours per week, work hours are trichotomized as less than forty hours, forty hours, and more than forty hours per week. Days worked per week are classified as one to four, five, and six to seven.

TABLE 6.3

Wife's Number of Hours Worked per Week by Husband's
Number of Hours Worked per Week[a]

Wife's Number of Hours Worked per Week	Husband's Numbers of Hours Worked per Week			All Categories
	<40	40	>40	
<40	44	72	118	234
	59.5%	46.2%	43.7%	46.8%
40	22	56	92	170
	29.7	35.9	34.1	34.0
>40	8	28	60	96
	10.8	17.9	22.2	19.2
All Categories[b]	74	156	270	500
	14.8	31.2	54.0	

[a]Difference between husband's and wife's distributions (comparison of row and column marginals): $X^2 = 166.6$, 2 df, $p < .001$; association between husband's and wife's hours/week: $X^2 = 5.96$, 4 df, ns.
[b]Percents add up to 100 across this row; all other percents are column percents.

TABLE 6.4

Wife's Number of Days Worked per Week by
Husband's Number of Days Worked per Week[a]

Wife's Number of Days Worked	Husband's Numbers of Days Worked			All Categories
	1–4 Days	5 Days	6–7 Days	
1–4 Days	8	70	17	95
	33.3%	19.7%	16.0%	19.6%
5 Days	13	254	66	333
	54.2	71.5	62.3	68.7
6–7 Days	3	31	23	57
	12.5	8.7	21.7	11.8
All Categories[b]	24	355	106	485
	4.9	73.2	21.9	

[a]Among couples in which both spouses work a regular number of days per week; difference between husband's and wife's distributions (comparison of row and column marginals): $X^2 = 56.7$, 2 df, $p < .001$; association between husband's and wife's days/week: $X^2 = 17.6$, 4 df, $p < .005$.
[b]Percents add up to 100 across this row; all other percents are column percents.

The finding that husbands start work earlier and end work later than their wives suggests that they work more total hours per week. Table 6.2 confirms this. While 54 percent of the husbands report working more than forty hours per week, only 19.2 percent of wives report the same; 14.8 percent of husbands say they work less than forty hours, compared to 46.8 percent of wives. Likewise, 21.9 percent of husbands work more than five days a week, in contrast to 11.8 percent of wives; only 4.9 percent of husbands work fewer than five days a week, while 19.6 percent of wives do so.

Husbands' and wives' number of days worked per week are positively correlated, so that they tend to have similar schedules; husbands working one to four days are particularly likely to have wives working one to four and so on. The same pattern of positive association holds for hours worked per week, though it does not attain statistical significance. Thus, at the within-couple level, husbands' and wives' amounts of time worked are similar rather than complementary. Husbands' and wives' times in paid work do not appear to substitute for or be interchangeable with each other. A husband working long hours does not appear to generate enough income to permit his wife to work shorter hours. Rather, a husband's long hours appear to indicate economic need or other factors which are likely to lead his wife to work long hours as well.

Second Jobs

As indicated in Table 6.5, 17.8 percent of the husbands and 9.2 percent of the wives in two-earner couples report holding a second job in addition to their main job, a statistically significant difference. At the same time, a husband with a second job is significantly more likely than the one-job husband to have a wife holding a second job (16.7 vs. 7.6 percent). Thus, second job holding shows a similar pattern of results as a high number of hours and days worked. This is more common in dual-earner husbands than wives, but at the within-couple level second job holding by husbands is positively associated with second job holding by their wives.

Summary

Our main findings concerning the aggregate distributions of husbands' and wives' schedules in two-earner couples are that husbands more often work on weekends, start their jobs earlier, end them later, work more hours per week, work more days per week, and more often hold second jobs. However, dual-earner husbands are not more likely

TABLE 6.5
Wife's Second Job by Husband's Second Job[a]

Wife	Husband		All Categories
	Has Second Job	No Second Job	
Has Second Job	15 16.7%	31 7.6%	46 9.2%
No Second Job	75 83.3	379 92.4	454 90.8
All Categories[b]	90 18.0	410 82.0	500

[a]Difference between husband's and wife's distributions (comparison of row and column marginals): Yates $X^2 = 15.5$, 1 df, $p < .001$; association between husband's and wife's second job status: Yates $X^2 = 8.46$, 1 df, $p < .01$.
[b]Percents add up to 100 across this row; all other percents are column percents.

than dual-earner wives to work nondaytime shifts. Thus, in all respects except shiftwork, husbands more often than wives work schedules which are potentially detrimental to their participation in family life.

At the within-couple level, husbands and wives have schedules which are positively correlated (rather than unrelated or complementary) in terms of pattern of days worked, amount of time worked, and holding a second job. In terms of work shift, however, husbands' and wives' schedules are unrelated. Shiftwork is the exception to the general pattern set by other schedule variables both in terms of the comparison of husbands' and wives' aggregate distributions and relationships at the within-couple level.

Husbands typically have more stressful schedules than wives judging by most criteria, but husbands whose schedules are more stressful than average for husbands are likely to have wives whose schedules are more stressful than average for wives. As a result, the implications of the overall sex differences in work schedules at the aggregate level are somewhat mitigated by relationships between husbands' and wives' schedules at the within-couple level. The one exception to the general pattern of within-couple association is work shift. However, this is also the one instance in which dual-earner wives' schedules are as potentially stressful as their husbands' at the individual level. Thus, the degree and implications of aggregate sex differences in schedules are less clearcut than they might first appear, particularly when couple-level patterns are examined.

Further, the positive association between spouses' schedules observed here indicates that the effects of an individual's and his or her spouse's schedule on the individual's family life may indeed be empirically confounded. Investigating the impact of either the individual's or the spouse's schedule on the individual's family life clearly requires controlling for the schedule of the other.

Couples' Joint Schedule Patterns and Their Correlates

Tables 6.1 to 6.5 provide information on the joint patterns of job schedules in two-earner couples. We will examine these joint schedule patterns and their correlates.

Pattern of Days Worked

Both husband and wife work a regular, nonweekend schedule in about 45 percent of all two-earner couples (Table 6.1). Either or both husband and wife (more often the husband only) regularly work on at least one weekend day each week in 34.4 percent of two-earner couples, including 5.6 percent in which both work weekends. Either or both work a variable number of days in 26.2 percent of the couples.

A six-category pattern variable was constructed representing the various possible combinations of spouses' pattern of days. As indicated in Table 6.6, this pattern variable was not significantly associated with the demographic variables examined here.

Shift

Both husband and wife work a day shift *(both day)* in 54.3 percent of the two-earner couples in the sample (Table 6.2). In 11.8 percent, one spouse has a regular day shift and the other has a nonday shift *(different shift)*, a figure comparable to Duncan and Hill's (1975) estimate of 16 percent. Interestingly, in this arrangement it is more often the wife than the husband (34 vs. 24 cases) who has the nonday shift. Considerably more frequent than the day/nonday combination is a third general pattern in which one spouse (and sometimes both) has a *variable* starting time, evident in 32.9 percent of the couples. Surprisingly, husbands are as likely as wives to be the spouse with the variable shift.

As shown in Table 6.7, couples' shift patterns are significantly related to family life-cycle stage. Couples with preschool children have the lowest proportion in the *both day* pattern (41.2 percent) and the highest proportions in the *different shift* pattern (21.0 percent) and the *variable* pattern (37.8 percent). Couples with older children show

TABLE 6.6

Couples' Patterns of Days Worked by Family Life-Cycle
Stage, Child-Care Use, Socioeconomic Status,[a] and Education[a]

Groups	Couples' Weekend/Variable Days Pattern[b]						
	Both Regular	Regular, Weekend	Both Weekend	Regular, Variable	Weekend, Variable	Both Variable	N
All	45.1%	23.2%	5.6%	17.4%	5.6%	3.2%	501
Family Life-Cycle Stage							
<45, No Children	44.0	22.0	3.3	18.7	4.4	7.7	91
Youngest 0–5	47.5	20.5	3.3	20.5	5.7	2.5	122
Youngest 6–12	50.8	23.3	5.8	12.5	5.0	2.5	120
Youngest 13–17	36.9	24.6	4.6	21.5	9.2	3.1	65
≥45, No Children	41.6	25.7	10.9	15.8	5.0	1.0	101
						p = ns	
Child-Care Use[c]							
User	58.3	20.4	1.9	12.0	3.7	3.7	108
Nonuser	42.1	24.1	6.0	19.5	6.8	1.5	133
						p < .07	
Socioeconomic Index							
White Collar	42.7	22.7	7.3	17.7	6.5	3.1	260
Blue Collar	47.7	23.7	3.7	17.0	4.6	3.3	241
						p = ns	
Education							
Less than H.S. Diploma	39.0	22.0	6.0	26.0	5.0	2.0	100
H.S. Diploma	48.7	23.3	6.2	13.0	5.7	3.1	193
Greater than H.S. Diploma	44.6	23.0	4.9	17.6	5.9	3.9	204
						p = ns	

[a]Respondent's.
[b]Percentages added up within rows.
[c]Among families with youngest child 0–12.

higher proportions in the *both day* pattern and lower proportions in
the other two. Those couples without children currently in the household appear to be split according to age: younger couples currently
living without children show a distribution of patterns similar to the
sample as a whole; older couples currently without children, however,
show a markedly high rate of the *both day* pattern (67.7 percent) and a
markedly low rate in the *different shift* pattern (3.0 percent).

Lein et al. (1974) hypothesized that formal child care arrangements
and the different shift pattern are alternative ways that parents of preschool children can meet their child care responsibilities. Table 6.7
shows that there is no significant association between the use of formal

child care and the couples' shift patterns. Parents of children aged twelve or under who use formal child care are as likely to show the *different shift* pattern as those not using formal childcare (17.8 vs. 18.6 percent). Testing Lein's hypothesis, however, requires examining the relationship between child care arrangements and couple shift pattern only for parents of preschool children, rather than the broader group of parents in Table 6.7. Analyses not shown here demonstrate that, among the subgroup of the 83 two-earner couples with a youngest child aged zero to five who have a formal child care arrangement, 15.7 percent are on different shifts. Only 36 couples in this subgroup do not use a formal child care arrangement, but among them 27.8 percent are on different shifts — the highest percentage in any subgroup. This supports Lein's hypothesis. The latter subgroup also registers the lowest percentage with both spouses on a regular day shift, 18.2 percent. Unfortunately, the sample size in this subgroup is so small that these percentages may be unreliable, and the difference between the two subgroups is not statistically significant.

Finally, couples with high socioeconomic status (as assessed by Duncan's Socioeconomic Index) and education are more likely to exhibit the *both day* pattern and less likely to show the other two patterns. The higher the status, the more likely they are to have this pattern; the different shift and variable shift patterns occur disproportionately among lower status and less educated couples.

Number of Hours

The most common pattern of number of hours worked per week is the husband working more than forty hours and the wife working less than forty. Almost one-quarter (23.6 percent) of the sample follow this pattern (Table 6.3). Other patterns in which the husband works more hours than the wife are also common, and all together constitute 56.4 percent of the sample. Husband and wife work a similar number of hours in 32.0 percent of the couples, and the wife works more hours in 11.6 percent.

In Table 6.8, these patterns are classified into six categories, representing the various combinations of spouses working less, exactly, or more than forty hours. The pattern is significantly associated with socioeconomic status and education, but the interpretation of this association is not clear. In couples in which workers have higher SEI scores, the spouses appear more likely to both be working more than forty hours per week. Differences in other categories are of smaller magnitude and inconsistent in direction. More educated couples also

TABLE 6.7

Couples' Shift Patterns by Family Life-Cycle
Stage, Child-Care Use, Socioeconomic Status,[a] and Education[a]

Groups	Couples' Shift Pattern[b]			N
	Both Day	Different Shift	Variable	
All	54.3%	12.2%	32.9%	492
Family Life-Cycle Stage				
<45, No Children	53.8	12.1	34.1	91
Youngest 0–5	41.2	21.0	37.8	119
Youngest 6–12	56.4	15.4	28.2	117
Youngest 13–17	53.8	9.2	36.9	65
≥45, No Children	67.7	3.0	29.3	99
			$p < .05$	
Child-Care Use[c]				
User	52.3	17.8	29.9	107
Nonuser	45.7	18.6	35.7	129
			ns	
Socioeconomic Index				
White Collar	58.8	9.4	31.8	255
Blue Collar	49.4	16.5	43.2	237
			$p < .05$	
Education				
Less than H.S. Diploma	48.0	16.3	35.7	98
H.S. Diploma	50.8	13.0	36.3	193
More than H.S. Diploma	61.1	11.1	27.8	198
			ns	

[a]Respondent's.
[b]Percentages added up within rows.
[c]Among families with youngest child 0–12.

are markedly high on this "both greater than forty" pattern, with other differences being less consistent.

Number of Days

The most common pattern of number of days worked per week is both spouses working exactly five days. This is the pattern for 52.3 percent of the couples (Table 6.4). All patterns in which husbands and wives work similar numbers of days constitute 58.8 percent of the sample; husbands work more days per week in 31.5 percent, and wives work more days in 9.7 percent.

The number of days patterns were also divided into six categories representing various combinations of spouses working less than, exactly,

TABLE 6.8

Couples' Number-of-Hours Patterns by Family Life-Cycle
Stage, Child-Care Use, Socioeconomic Status,[a] and Education[a]

Groups	Couples' Number of Hours Pattern[b]						N
	Both <40	<40 40	<40 >40	Both 40	40 >40	Both >40	
All	9.4%	19.4%	25.6%	11.7%	23.5%	10.4%	481
Family Life-Cycle Stage							
<45, No Children	12.2	20.0	15.6	10.1	26.7	15.6	90
Youngest 0–5	10.3	23.3	29.3	11.2	17.2	8.6	116
Youngest 6–12	8.5	17.1	25.6	12.8	29.9	6.0	117
Youngest 13–17	9.7	12.9	32.3	11.3	22.6	11.3	62
≥45, No Children	6.3	21.1	26.3	12.6	21.1	12.6	95
						p = ns	
Child-Care Use [c]							
User	8.5	18.9	25.5	18.9	20.8	7.5	106
Nonuser	10.2	21.3	29.1	6.3	26.0	7.1	127
						p = .11	
Socioeconomic Index							
White Collar	10.1	15.4	27.9	8.1	22.3	16.2	247
Blue Collar	8.5	23.5	23.1	15.4	25.4	4.3	234
						p .001	
Education							
Less than H.S. Diploma	6.3	28.4	20.0	16.8	21.1	7.4	95
H.S. Diploma	6.3	19.6	27.5	13.2	27.5	5.8	189
Greater than H.S. Diploma	13.4	14.4	26.3	7.7	21.6	16.5	194
						p .001	

[a]Respondent's.
[b]Percentages added up within rows.
[c]Among families with youngest child 0–12.

or more than five days per week. This pattern variable shows significant association only with the use of formal child care among families with children aged twelve and younger (Table 6.9). When such families use formal child care, they more frequently have both spouses working exactly five days a week and less often use all other patterns.

Second Jobs

Either the husband or the wife holds a second job in 24.2 percent of two-earner couples (Table 6.5). The husband is somewhat more than twice as likely as his wife to be the one holding the second job, if only

TABLE 6.9

Couples' Number-of-Days Patterns by Family Life-Cycle
Stage, Child-Care Use, Socioeconomic Status,[a] and Education[a]

Groups	Both <5	5 <5	Both 5	<5 5	5 >5	Both >5	N
			Couples' Number of Days Pattern[b]				
All	1.6%	17.1%	52.4%	4.1%	20.0%	4.7%	485
Family Life-Cycle Stage							
<45, No Children	2.3	10.5	60.5	1.2	23.3	2.3	86
Youngest 0–5	2.5	20.0	55.0	4.2	15.0	3.3	120
Youngest 6–12	0.9	15.4	53.8	4.3	21.4	4.3	117
Youngest 13–17	3.2	14.5	48.4	4.8	21.0	8.1	62
≥45, No Children	0.0	23.2	43.4	6.1	20.2	7.1	99
						p = ns	
Child-Care Use[c]							
User	0.9	15.0	66.4	3.7	12.1	1.9	107
Nonuser	2.3	20.0	44.6	3.8	23.8	5.4	130
						p<.05	
Socioeconomic Index							
White Collar	1.2	16.2	49.8	4.7	20.6	7.5	253
Blue Collar	2.2	18.1	55.2	3.4	19.4	1.7	232
						p<.06	
Education							
Less than H.S. Diploma	1.1	16.0	54.3	5.3	19.1	4.3	94
H.S. Diploma	2.1	15.3	51.6	4.2	21.1	5.8	190
Greater than H.S. Diploma	1.5	19.2	52.5	3.5	19.2	4.0	198
						p = ns	

[a]Respondent's.
[b]Percentages added up within rows.
[c]Among families with youngest child 0–12.

one does. *Both* husband and wife hold second jobs in 3.0 percent of the couples in the sample.

Family life-cycle stage significantly influences which pattern a couple follows (Table 6.10). Young couples without children show the highest rates of one or both partner having a second job (36.3 percent). As couples go through the family life cycle, the rates of one or both spouses holding a second job steadily decline, so that in older, presumably post-parental couples without children, only 14.9 percent have second jobs held by either or both partners.

TABLE 6.10

Couples' Second Job Patterns by Family Life-Cycle
Stage, Child-Care Use, Socioeconomic Status,[a] and Education[a]

Groups	Couple Second Job Pattern[b]			
	Neither Has Second Job	One Has Second Job	Both Have Second Job	N
All	75.4%	21.6%	3.0%	499
Family Life-Cycle Stage				
<45, No Children	63.7	28.6	7.7	91
Youngest 0–5	71.3	25.4	3.3	122
Youngest 6–12	74.8	23.5	1.7	119
Youngest 13–17	84.6	13.8	1.5	65
≥45, No Children	85.1	13.9	1.0	101
		$p < .01$		
Child-Care Use[c]				
User	75.0	23.1	1.9	108
Nonuser	72.0	25.0	3.0	132
		p = ns		
Socioeconomic Index				
White Collar	73.5	22.7	3.8	260
Blue Collar	77.4	20.5	2.1	237
		p = ns		
Education				
Less than H.S. Diploma	90.9	9.1	0.0	99
H.S. Diploma	77.7	20.2	2.1	193
Greater than H.S. Diploma	65.7	28.9	5.4	204
		$p < .001$		

[a]Respondent's.
[b]Percentages added up within rows.
[c]Among families with youngest child 0–12.

Couples' second job pattern shows no significant covariation with child-care use or socioeconomic status, but is strongly related to education. The more educated the couple, the more likely it is that one or both spouses have a second job — only 9.1 percent of couples with less than a high school diploma do, compared to 34.3 percent of those with any education beyond a high school diploma. Education and youth are, of course, positively related, and it was not feasible to disentangle their effects in this analysis. It is possible that holding a second job is related to the relatively low earning power and the higher level of energy associated with youth, rather than high level of education *per se.*

Summary

Our main findings concerning two-earner couples' joint schedule patterns and their correlates are as follows:
1. Either or both husband and wife regularly work on at least one weekend day in 34.4 percent of the couples. Either or both work a variable number of days in 26.2 percent. These patterns appear unrelated to demographic variables.
2. In 54.3 percent of the couples, both spouses work regular daytime shifts, spouses work different shifts on a regular basis in 12.2 percent, and one or both spouses has a variable starting time in 32.9 percent. These patterns are related to demographic variables. In particular, the different shift pattern is most common in families with preschoolers, and the different shift and variable patterns are most common in families of lower social status.
3. Husbands work longer hours than their wives on the average. However, both spouses work a similar number of hours in 32.0 percent of the couples and the wife works more hours in 11.6 percent. Both spouses working more than forty hours a week is associated with high education and high socioeconomic status.
4. Both husbands and wives work exactly five days a week in 52.3 percent of the couples. Husbands work more days than their wives in 31.5 percent and fewer in 9.7 percent.
5. Either or both husband and wife holds a second job in 24.2 percent of all dual-earner couples, including 3.0 percent in which both spouses do. One or both spouses holding a second job is associated with being young and with being highly educated.

Main Effects of Husbands' and
Wives' Work Schedules on Family Life

Tables 6.11 and 6.12 present the regression results concerning the effects of husbands' and wives' work schedules on the family life of each of them. The effects of each work schedule characteristic on family life in the larger analysis sample examined in Chapter 4 are briefly re-counted as a context for the results specific to dual-earner husbands and wives presented here. The direction and magnitude of effects within dual-earner couples are then discussed. Differences between parallel effects in husbands and wives are not statistically significant unless otherwise noted.

Pattern of Days Worked

In the larger analysis sample examined in Chapter 4, schedules including regular weekend work are associated with decreased time in child care and housework and increased hours conflict and schedule conflict. Working a variable number of days each week predicts less time in child care, more schedule conflict, and decreased family adjustment.

Regular weekend work reduces time in child care and housework to a significant degree among dual-earner husbands but not among dual-earner wives. Dual-earner husbands may ordinarily "catch up" on housework and child care on the weekend, performing a relatively high proportion of their weekly total during this period; regular weekend work appears to interfere with husbands' contributions. Weekend work has small effects in opposite directions on the various indicators of work/family conflict among husbands and wives, but none of the individual coefficients is statistically significant. Working a variable number of days has weak, nonsignificant, but somewhat variable effects in husbands and wives.

Two significant "cross-over" effects are evident. First, the wife working a variable number of days each week reduces husband's time in housework. Interestingly, this same characteristic has a nonsignificant, negative effect on the wife's own housework time. Second, a husband's regular weekend work is associated with a significant elevation in his wife's reports of schedule conflict (though not his own).

Shift

In the larger analysis sample, nondaytime and variable shifts were associated with more time in housework, but also with higher levels of total work/family conflict and conflict specifically concerning scheduling. In two-earner couples, nondaytime work predicts significantly high levels of housework for both husband and wife. It predicts significantly elevated total and schedule conflict, however, only for husbands. Variable schedules are significantly associated with hours conflict only among husbands.

One cross-over effect attains statistical significance: a wife's nondaytime schedule significantly increases her husband's experience of schedule conflict. It increases her own experience of total work/family conflict to almost the same degree, but not at a statistically significant level. By contrast, husbands' nondaytime work affects wives' schedule conflict to a much smaller degree.

TABLE 6.11

Metric Regression Coefficients for Net Additive Effects of Husbands' and Wives' Work Schedule Characteristics on Husbands' Family Measures

Demographic Controls and Work Schedule Characteristics (Indep. Var.)	Family Measures (Dep. Var.)					
	Time in Child Care	Time in Housework	Total Conflict	Hours Conflict	Schedule Conflict	Family Adjustment
Demographic Controls						
Family Life-Cycle Stage						
Youngest Child under 6	—[a]	2.696	.228	.162	.046	-.316
Youngest Child 6–12	-5.289	3.219	.210	.148	-.053	-.425*
Youngest Child 13–17	-15.274**	1.383	.094	.009	-.067	-.453
Childless, 45 or Older	—[a]	9.253	-.155	-.102	-.033	-.157
(Omitted Category: Childless, under 45)						
Education	-.827	-.652	.058	.002	-.003	-.090
Duncan SEI	-.007	-.005	.010	.021	-.006	.000
Formal Child Care Arrangements	-1.909	-1.607	-.168	-.139	-.009	.007
Work Schedule Characteristics						
Pattern of Days Worked						
Husband – Regular, Weekend	-5.965*	-7.025**	.213	.141	.037	.068
Husband – Variable Days	.089	1.097	-.041	-.162	.096	-.209
Wife – Regular, Weekend	-.046	-1.341	-.053	-.092	.021	-.108
Wife – Variable Days	.131	-3.837*	.069	.075	-.054	-.204
(Omitted Categories: Husband – Regular, Nonweekend; Wife – Regular, Nonweekend)						
Shift						
Husband – Nonday	2.625	7.780**	.497*	.064	.399**	-.121
Husband – Variable	4.280	-.607	.254	.224*	.122	.088

TABLE 6.11 (Continued)

Demographic Controls and Work Schedule Characteristics (Indep. Var.)	Family Measures (Dep. Var.)					
	Time in Child Care	Time in Housework	Total Conflict	Hours Conflict	Schedule Conflict	Family Adjustment
Wife—Nonday	6.001	1.538	.237	.029	.227*	-.155
Wife—Variable	-.931	.596	-.013	.048	.114	-.094
(Omitted Categories: Husband—Day; Wife—Day)						
Number of Hours Worked						
Husband—Hours	.003	-.099	.018**	.009**	.002	-.002
Wife—Hours	-.009	-.015	-.007	-.001	.008	-.005
Second Job						
Husband—Second Job	-1.526	.598	-.124	-.058	-.018	-.032
Wife—Second Job	-4.932	-2.16	.205	.206	.003	-.247
Adjusted R^2 Explained By:						
Demographic Controls	.2024	.0268	.0143	.0094	.0116	.0315
Work Schedule Characteristics	-.0023	.0891	.0793	.0471	.0939	.0205
All Variables	.2001	.1159	.0936	.0565	.1055	.0520
N	145	247	247	247	247	247

*p<.05.
**p<.01.
aFor time in child care, those without children were excluded from the analysis, and the omitted category becomes parents whose youngest child is under 6.

TABLE 6.12

Metric Regression Coefficients for Net Additive Effects of Wives' and
Husbands' Work Schedule Characteristics on Wives' Family Measures

Demographic Controls and Work Schedule Characteristics (Indep. Var.)	Family Measures (Dep. Var.)					
	Time in Child Care	Time in Housework	Total Conflict	Hours Conflict	Schedule Conflict	Family Adjustment
Demographic Controls						
Family Life-Cycle Stage						
Youngest Child under 6	—[a]	10.850**	.205	.054	-.002	-.238
Youngest Child 6–12	-11.645**	9.087***	.125	.161	-.032	-.279
Youngest Child 13–17	-22.223***	6.925	.125	-.022	-.056	-.337
Childless, 45 or Older	—[a]	7.837**	-.474	-.120	.120	-.175
(Omitted Category: Childless, under 45)						
Education	2.386	.067	-.063	-.033	-.045	.053
Duncan SEI	.016**	.003	-.002	-.001	-.001	.000
Formal Child Care Arrangements	-.283	-2.615***	.201	-.020	-.019	.039
Work Schedule Characteristics						
Pattern of Days Worked						
Wife—Regular, Weekend	-3.761*	-2.142	-.199	-.118	.110	.025
Wife—Variable Days	-4.841	-2.053	-.216	-.060	.005	-.269
Husband—Regular, Weekend	-.745	.443	.035	-.082	.147*	-.095
Husband—Variable Days	9.002	3.059	-.038	-.125	.018	.189
(Omitted Categories: Wife—Regular, Nonweekend; Husband—Regular, Nonweekend)						
Shift						
Wife—Nonday	6.711	8.378*	.281	-.030	.195	.016
Wife—Variable	-1.728	1.878	.332	.048	.019	.129

TABLE 6.12 (Continued)

Demographic Controls and Work Schedule Characteristics (Indep. Var.)	Family Measures (Dep. Var.)					
	Time in Child Care	Time in Housework	Total Conflict	Hours Conflict	Schedule Conflict	Family Adjustment
Husband–Nonday	−.159	−4.378	.278	−.062	.094	.240
Husband–Variable	−.522	−4.545	.298	.078	.000	−.218
(Omitted Categories: Wife–Day; Husband–Day)						
Number of Hours Worked						
Wife–Hours	−.521**	−.268**	.029**	.021**	−.002	−.001
Husband–Hours	.068	.041	.001	.001	−.002	.000
Second Job						
Wife–Second Job	.376	.587	.133	.202*	.103	−.415**
Husband–Second Job	.452	.075	−.066	−.028	−.037	−.086
Adjusted R² Explained By:						
Demographic Controls	.2790	.0649	.0844	.0107	−.0120	−.0152
Work Schedule Characteristics	.1068	.0554	.0861	.1484	.0232	.0412
All Variables	.3858	.1203	.1705	.1591	.0112	.0260
N	126	211	211	211	211	211

*p < .05.
**p < .01.
[a]For time in child care, those without children were excluded from the analysis, and the omitted category becomes parents whose youngest child is under 6.

Number of Hours

In the full sample, working long hours predicted decreases in house-work time and increases in total work/family conflict. In two-earner couples, number of hours worked has a significantly stronger negative effect on time in child care and housework for wives than for husbands; further, the effect is significant among the former but not the latter. Number of hours worked also has significantly stronger effects on total and hours conflict among wives than husbands, though these effects are significant within both sexes. No cross-over effects are evident, however.

Second Jobs

This variable was not examined in the full sample. Among dual-earner wives, second jobs predict higher levels of hours conflict and lower levels of family adjustment. Interestingly, a wife holding a second job is also associated with decreased family adjustment as reported by the husband, though not to a significant degree. By con-trast, a husband holding a second job has only negligible effects on the family adjustment of either spouse.

Summary and Discussion

Several effects of an individual's work schedule characteristics on his or her family life which are significant for the full sample are not sig-nificant for dual-earner husbands and wives. To some extent, this occurs because the smaller N's in the dual-earner group require larger effects to attain significance. Further, the introduction of controls on spouses' schedule characteristics makes tests of the effects of individ-uals' schedule characteristics more conservative.

In our analysis, certain work schedule characteristics appear to have significant effects on aspects of an individual's family life when they occur among husbands but not among wives. These include the neg-ative effect of weekend work on time in child care and housework, and the effect of shiftwork on work/family conflict as a whole and specifi-cally scheduling. Other schedule characteristics appear to have signifi-cant effects among wives but not among husbands: the effect of number of hours worked on time in child care and housework, and the effect of second jobs on hours conflict and family adjustment. It is intriguing that an individual's family life appears generally more responsive to number of hours worked among wives, but to shift and pattern of days worked among husbands. (The exception is that non-daytime shiftwork has quite similar effects among husbands and wives in increasing time in housework.)

These results differ from those of earlier studies in two aspects. First, whereas Robinson's (1977) data suggest that time in work affects time in family roles more for men than for women, our data show that the negative relationship between the two is stronger among women than men. Second, Keith and Schafer (1980) found that time at the job predicted work/family conflict better among men than women; our data show the opposite. Our data do not replicate the cross-over effects observed in previous research, such as Walker and Woods's (1976) finding concerning the impact of a husband's work hours on his wife's housework and Keith and Schafer's (1980) finding on the effects of the husband's hours on his wife's level of conflict.

They do, however, reveal three cross-over effects which have not been observed previously. Two of these effects reveal an interesting asymmetry. First, husbands experience schedule conflict when their wives work nondaytime shifts. Wives are not equally sensitive to shiftwork by their husbands. Second, wives experience elevated schedule conflict when their husbands work on weekends, but husbands do not have a similar reaction to wives' weekend work. This asymmetrical pattern may be interpretable in light of the effects of these schedule characteristics on husbands' and wives' time use. When a husband works a nondaytime shift, he increases his housework, thus taking over some of his wife's traditional family responsibility. Therefore, a wife's conflict is not significantly increased by her husband's shiftwork. But a husband's weekend work does significantly reduce his time in child care and housework, since he may use weekends to "catch up" on these activities. In this circumstance, the wife's conflicts are increased. By contrast, a wife's weekend work leads to only small, nonsignificant decreases in her own time in family roles and to little change in her husband's. Thus, the husband's conflict is not elevated; the wife's shiftwork appears to increase his time in child care. Though this increment is not statistically significant, it appears to be an additional family responsibility that causes the husband to experience more conflict. Interestingly, in both these interpretations, the cross-over effects of one spouse's schedule on the other's work/family conflict is mediated by the effects of the first spouse's schedule (whether the husband or wife) on the husband's performance of housework or child care.

The third cross-over effect has no clear interpretation: husbands do less housework when their wives work a variable number of days each week.

Interactive Effects of Husbands' and Wives' Schedules on Family Life

Analyses were also conducted to investigate how husbands' and wives' schedules interact to influence the family life of either of them. Following the procedures for testing interaction effects presented earlier, only one set of effects was found to be significant: interactions between husbands' and wives' shifts on husbands' schedule conflict.

As shown in Table 6.13, the overall pattern is that the effects of a husband's nonday and variable shifts on his reports of schedule conflict are usually exacerbated when his wife also has a nonday or variable shift.[1] The one exception is that a husband's nonday shift does not have a significantly stronger impact on his schedule conflict when his wife has a variable shift than when she works a regular day shift. Even in this case, however, the effect of the husband's nonday shift is substantially (though nonsignificantly) elevated.

It appears that the detrimental impact of the husband's nonday shift is intensified even further when the wife has a nonday or variable shift. A husband's variable shift, which has no significant effect on his schedule conflict either overall or when his wife works a day shift, is associated with significantly increased schedule conflict when his wife works a nonday or variable shift. According to Table 6.2, these combinations of nonday and/or variable shifts with this heightened impact on husbands occur in about 8.9 percent of all two-earner couples.

It is intriguing that, at least in terms of avoiding schedule conflict, a variable shift appears to be compatible with a day shift, but not with another variable or nonday shift. It is also noteworthy that these shift interactions do not appear to influence a wife's experience of conflict to a significant degree.

Summary

Comparing two-earner couples' schedules in the aggregate, husbands' schedules are more demanding in all respects except the frequency of shiftwork. At the within-couple level, husbands' and wives' schedules tend to be correlated on most schedule characteristics, with shift again being the exception.

Examination of couple-level patterns of schedules revealed several noteworthy findings. Either or both spouses work at least one weekend day a week on a regular basis in just over one-third of all dual-earner couples. In about 12 percent, one spouse works a day shift and the other works some other regular shift. This "different shift" pattern is

TABLE 6.13

Conditioning Effect of Wife's Shift on Relationship
between Husband's Shift and Schedule Conflict

Husband's Shift	Effect of Husband's Shift When Wife's Shift is:[a]			Main Effect	Increment to R^2 Due to Interaction
	Day	Nonday	Variable		
Nonday	.289	.943*	.575	.399*	.0770*
Variable	− .012	.869*	.466**	.123	

*p < .05.
**p < .01.
[a]Significance levels of regression coefficients for interaction refer to comparisons between the category indicated and the referent category (wife day shift).

particularly common in families with preschool children, especially if no formal child care arrangement is used, and also occurs disproportionately in families of lower socioeconomic status. In nearly one-quarter of two-earner families, particularly young and highly educated families, one or both spouses holds a second job.

Among dual-earner husbands, weekend work reduces time in child care and housework, and shiftwork increases total work/family conflict and schedule conflict. Among dual-earner wives, long hours worked per week reduce time in housework and child care and increase total and hours conflict; second jobs increase hours conflict and reduce family adjustment. Shiftwork appears to be associated with increased time in housework for both husbands and wives.

While certain cross-over effects noted in previous research were not replicated in these data, several other cross-over effects are evident. Dual-earner husbands experience more schedule conflict when their wives do shiftwork, while dual-earner wives register increased schedule conflict when their husbands work regularly on weekends. Husbands also perform less housework if their wives work a variable number of days each week.

Finally, a significant interaction was observed in the joint effects of husbands' and wives' shiftwork on husbands' degree of schedule conflict. The negative effects of a husband's shiftwork on his schedule conflict are exacerbated when his wife also has shiftwork or a variable starting time. A husband's variable shifts are not associated with elevated schedule conflict if his wife has a regular day shift, but do appear to increase his conflict if his wife has shiftwork or a variable shift.

Note

1. These interaction effects could be alternatively displayed as differential effects of the wife's shift under the circumstance of the husband having a day, nonday, or variable shift. The implication is the same: when both husband and wife have a nonday or variable shift, the husband's schedule conflict is particularly high.

7

Summary and Conclusions

This study investigates the impact of work schedules on family life. It goes beyond previous research in terms of comprehensiveness of sample, measures, and analytic strategy. In so doing, it raises and addresses a variety of technical issues of methodology and generates a number of empirical findings. This final chapter summarizes and discusses those findings and spells out their implications for new directions in future research and social policy.

Main Effects of Work Schedule Characteristics

Chapter 3 contains preliminary information on the distributions of scores for two major sets of measures: work schedule characteristics associated with workers' main jobs and dimensions of the quality of family life. An extensive analysis of the main effects of work schedule characteristics on the quality of family life appears in Chapter 4. Based on multiple regression, the analysis tests three hypotheses regarding main effects.

Summary of Findings

Distributional information. Just over three-fifths of the workers in the sample work a regular pattern of weekdays with no weekend work. Women prove more likely to work a regular pattern of weekdays and men tend to engage in more weekend work. Almost three-quarters of the workers work a regular day shift, with men and women equally likely to be on regular days. Men, however, work appreciably more hours each week than do women.

Workers report spending more time with their children (parents only) than on housework (all workers). Compared to employed men, employed women average twice as much time with their children and two-and-a-half times as much time on housework. One-third of all workers report that their job and their family life interfere with each other "somewhat" or "a lot." Sex makes no difference in overall level of work/family conflict although working men are more likely than working women to complain about excessive work hours interfering with family life and working women are more likely to mention scheduling conflicts. Workers offer highly positive assessments of their marriages and family life but men sound an even more positive theme than do women.

Pattern of days. The first hypothesis states that working a nonstandard pattern of days each week (weekend work, variable days) relates negatively to measures of the quality of family life. The multivariate analyses adduce considerable support for this initial hypothesis. According to the data, working nonstandard days is associated with less time in family roles, higher levels of specific types of work/family interference and, in one instance, lower family adjustment. It bears emphasis, nonetheless, that only about half of the combinations of measures of nonstandard days and family life generate significant regression coefficients; however, all of the significant relationships so generated do conform to the direction predicted by our first hypothesis. Unfortunately, other studies have not systematically tested this hypothesis; thus comparison of these results with those from other studies proves impossible.

Shift. According to the second hypothesis, working a nonstandard pattern of hours each day (afternoon, night, or rotating shift; variable hours) is negatively related to the quality of the worker's family life. Unlike the findings for the preceding hypothesis, the regression data linking shiftwork and family life provide only partial support for hypothesis 2. The data establish that nonday shifts permit *more* time in one family role (housework), yet also *more* work/family conflict. Moreover, shiftwork proves unrelated to time spent in the other family role (child care) and also unrelated to level of family adjustment. Other studies using multivariate analyses have confirmed the connection between shiftwork and greater work/family conflict but, curiously, have not explored the relationship between shiftwork and either time in family roles or level of family adjustment.

It is, admittedly, surprising that shiftwork does not reduce time spent in the two family roles studied and does not affect family adjustment at all. We offer only a tentative explanation as to why shiftwork relates positively to amount of time devoted to housework, namely, that many types of housework may be performed at any time of the day, so shiftworkers may choose to engage in home chores when their atypical work schedules exclude them from other, more structured, less flexible activities.

Interpretations of unanticipated findings aside, there is a central point to be emphasized here. The problems that shiftwork poses for family life appear to concern the scheduling, not the amount, of available time; and the time that shiftworkers have available for family members and family roles appears to come at the wrong period of the day. Quality of family time, in short, should not be confused with quantity of family time, and shiftwork is associated with lower quality of family time.

Number of hours worked. The third hypothesis posits a negative relationship between the number of hours worked each week and the quality of the worker's family life. According to the regression data, number of hours worked produces significant relationships with only two of the measures of family life. A high number of hours worked is associated with less time spent on housework and more total work/ family conflict. These two significant relationships clearly conform to the direction predicted by hypothesis 3 but no significant relationships emerge between number of hours worked and either time devoted to child care or level of family adjustment. Previously reported multivariate studies replicate the connection between long hours and high work/family conflict and also the absence of a connection between long hours and family adjustment. Consistency of evidence notwithstanding, it remains impressive but puzzling that workers do not allow long working hours to interfere with the amount of time they spend with their children or with their level of family adjustment.

Interpretation of Findings

Issues of reliability and validity of measures bear on the interpretation of data testing the first three (as well as later) hypotheses. Our analyses, unfortunately, provide little relevant psychometric information. Some of the measures of work schedule characteristics and family life, for example, contain only a single item. The other measures, with one exception, do not consist of homogeneous multi-item indices whose internal consistency may be computed. The exception, the three-item index of family adjustment enjoys a high level of internal consistency (alpha = .86). Other studies give us little exact information about the reliability and validity of the current measures, most of which are unique to the present investigation. We do know, however, that time estimates typically produce inflated figures when compared to the more precise data from time diaries; and we hypothesize that respondents also inflate their reports of family adjustment, which are highly skewed in a negative direction (i.e., mainly very favorable reports). These latter two types of inflated figures represent systematic errors (or biases) in the present measures and thus at the very least lower coefficients of validity. It does not seem possible, however, to make precise adjustments to the regression coefficients in order to compensate for the imperfect reliability and validity of measures, nor even to indicate whether various regression coefficients should be adjusted in either a positive or negative direction.

A further major issue raised by the data on main effects concerns causal direction. In principle, relationships between work schedule characteristics and family life invite a number of causal interpretations. Work schedules may causally affect family life or, alternatively, family life may causally affect work schedules. A third possibility is that some other factor (or set of factors) related to both work schedules and family life accounts for the relationship between them and thus renders the original relationship spurious. In all likelihood, however, the causal pattern in question is less of an all-or-nothing issue and more a matter of degree. That is, work schedules may cause variations in family life to some degree; family life may cause variations in work schedules to some degree; and spurious factors may also play some role.

As used in the present analyses, the regression procedure lends itself to certain causal interpretations rather than to others. It directly accommodates (and provides parameter estimates for) the causal view that work schedules affect family life since it treats work schedule characteristics as independent variables and family measures as dependent variables. The regression procedure also allows for and eliminates the possibility that certain demographic control variables act as spurious causes of the relationships between work schedule characteristics and family life, although other types of spurious relationships are not addressed. Importantly, the procedure as used does *not* entertain the possibility that family life affects work schedules.

We take the substantive position that the causal impact of work schedules on family life probably exceeds that of family life on work schedules. Our reasoning is that people have much less control over their work schedules than over their family lives and, thus, their family lives tend to adjust to their work schedules rather than the reverse. Evidence cited in Chapter 5 indicates how little capacity workers have to change their work schedules, although the convenience of work schedules does represent one factor that workers take into account when selecting a job in the first place. Because a basic (OLS) regression model effectively allows only one causal direction, we have implemented the regression strategy on the assumption that work schedules affect family life. Actually, we believe that family life may also have a causal impact on work schedules, and we advocate the future use of those statistical procedures (nonrecursive causal modeling techniques including two-stage least squares) that examine both causal directions. In short, we view the current regression data as probably oversimplifying the true causal pattern but nonetheless providing a useful first approximation.

Moderator Effects of Schedule Control

A number of factors may act as moderators of the relationships between work schedules and family life. Chapter 5 reports on tests of interaction based on four possible moderators: schedule control and three demographic factors (type of worker, family life-cycle stage, and education). As noted earlier, the testing procedure consists of a sequence of three steps (protected t strategy, counting strategy, and the criterion of substantive significance) designed to control Type I errors.

Summary of Findings

Of the four potential moderators, only schedule control survives the complete sequence of tests. The data on schedule control as a moderator directly test hypothesis 4 according to which the negative relationships between nonstandard work schedules and the quality of family life will be strongest when workers have least control over their work schedules. The actual analyses described in Chapter 5 uncover a series of conditioning effects generally in line with the fourth hypothesis. To be specific, whereas working an afternoon shift decreases time spent with children under low schedule control, it increases parental time under medium schedule control and increases it even more under high schedule control. Similarly, under conditions of low schedule control, working a night shift increases time in child care only slightly but the increase is substantial under high schedule control. The positive effect of number of hours worked per week on hours conflict, moreover, is greater under low than high schedule control; and regular weekend work increases schedule conflict under low schedule control, yet decreases such conflict under high schedule control. Here, then, are several concrete examples of how schedule control, functioning as a moderator variable, improves the effects of nonstandard work schedules on family life.

Interpretation of Findings

Other studies of the relationship between work schedules and family life have failed to use schedule control as a moderator variable, thereby eliminating the possibility of direct comparisons between present and previous findings. Existing literature does raise the issue of a relationship between schedule control and family life but only in the context of flextime, a special type of schedule that allows the worker a modest amount of flexibility as to starting (and hence ending) time of work. As reported in Chapter 2, investigations of flextime have compared the family life of workers on flexible schedules with the family life of other workers. Such investigations, in essence, examine the main effects of flexibility of starting time and do not explore whether such flexibility conditions the relationships between other work schedule characteristics and dimensions of family life. Our study treats flexibility (or schedule control) as a general dimension of work schedules that encompasses more than starting and ending times rather than as a simple dichotomous (or typological) classification such as flextime; and we examine the main effects of this general dimension on family life in conjunction with its conditioning effects on the relationship between work schedule characteristics and family life.

While our analysis uncovers several cases in which schedule control moderates the relationship between work schedules and family life, it does not detect a large number of such interactions. That is, many more of the possible interactions between schedule control and work schedule characteristics prove nonsignificant than significant. A series of factors suggest that the procedure used for testing interactions lacks statistical power and may thus allow a high rate of Type II errors. In the first place, the index of schedule control generates only a marginally satisfactory coefficient of internal reliability (alpha = .58). Moreover, because of the high collinearity between main and interaction terms in the relevant equations, tests of interaction in the moderated regression strategy typically lack high statistical power. In short, there are grounds for believing that under more favorable conditions of measurement and analysis, schedule control would emerge as a more powerful moderator of relationships between work schedules and family life.

A Special Sample: Dual-Earner Couples

This study gives special attention in Chapter 6 to families in which both husband and wife work for pay and in which, therefore, two separate work schedules can affect each person's experience of family life. The study thus takes advantage of the fact that interviewers asked all members of dual-earner couples to describe their spouse's work schedules as well as their own.

Summary of Findings

Comparisons between the job schedules of working husbands and working wives may take place at either the aggregate or within-couple level. In the aggregate, husbands have work schedules that make greater demands on them in virtually all respects except the frequency of shiftwork. Specifically, husbands work more often on weekends, average longer hours each week, and are more likely to have a second job. At the within-couple level, husbands' and wives' schedules tend to correlate positively on most schedule characteristics, with shift again being the exception. That is, husbands who work on weekends, variable days, long hours, or a second job tend to have wives who do the same. It bears emphasizing that comparisons between the schedules of spouses produce no relationships at all in the case of shiftwork. In other words, in the subsample of dual-earner couples, the sexes do not have different rates of nondaytime shifts at the aggregate level, nor do husbands and wives tend to have similar or dissimilar shifts at the within-couple level.

Chapter 6 also provides information on the joint pattern of job schedules in two-earner couples. Either or both spouses work at least one weekend day per week as part of their regular schedule in roughly one-third of all dual-earner couples. Both husband and wife work a day shift in somewhat more than half the dual-earner couples. In about one family in eight, one spouse works a day shift and the other works a nonday shift. This "different shift" pattern appears with greater frequency among families with preschool children, especially in the absence of any formal child care arrangement and is also frequent among those families with lower levels of education. Couples in which both spouses work long hours (i.e., the 12 percent in which both husband and wife work over forty hours a week) tend to have higher levels of education. Either the husband or the wife holds a second job in approximately one-quarter of two-earner couples. As couples progress through the family life-cycle, the rates of one or both spouses holding a second job decline; moreover, the better educated the couple, the more likely it is that one or both spouses hold a second job.

Paralleling the results on the main sample reported in Chapter 4, Chapter 6 details the main effects of work schedules on family life for the special sample of dual earners. Although the findings from the two analyses are broadly consistent, the pattern of significant relationships differs in a number of respects for husbands and wives in dual-earner couples. Among husbands, for example, weekend work reduces time spent in both child care and housework; second jobs constrain time with children; and shiftwork enhances both total work/family conflict and schedule conflict. Among dual-earner wives, by comparison, long weekly hours of work diminish time allocated to housework and child care and increase total and hours conflict; second jobs lead to increased hours conflict and reduced family adjustment. On the other hand, shiftwork is associated with more time devoted to housework among both husbands and wives.

Still in the context of main effects, the analyses in Chapter 6 also explore for patterns of cross-over effects, that is, evidence that one spouse's work schedule has a bearing on the other's family life, controlling for the first spouse's work schedule. Previous research has given preliminary indication that a husband's work schedule may have more impact on his wife's family life than a wife's schedule has on her husband's family life. The present findings do not replicate the tentative earlier pattern, however. Instead, they identify several specific cross-over effects. Dual-earner husbands register more schedule conflict when their wives work shifts whereas dual-earner wives experience increased schedule conflict when their husbands do regular weekend work. In addition, husbands report doing less housework if their wives work a variable number of days each week.

Finally, Chapter 6 tests for interactions between the respondent's and spouse's work schedules in the determination of the quality of the respondent's family life. Only one such interaction emerges from the testing based on the dual-earner sample. It concerns the joint effects of husbands' and wives' shiftwork on husbands' level of schedule conflict. The negative effects of a husband's shiftwork on his schedule conflict increase when his wife works either on a shift or on a variable pattern of hours. A husband's variable shift is not associated with enhanced schedule conflict if his wife has a regular day shift, but does appear to increase his conflict if his wife does shiftwork or works a variable pattern of hours.

Interpretation of Findings

From a methodological standpoint, much of what was said earlier about the findings for the main sample applies to the findings for the special sample of two-earner couples. For example, the method used to detect interactions suffers from insufficient statistical power, and to an undetermined degree, unreliability and invalidity of measures either diminish or distort significant relationships.

Certain other methodological considerations apply specifically to the analyses of the special sample of dual-earner families. The reduction in sample size makes statistical significance more difficult to obtain. The somewhat greater number of dual-earner husbands than dual-earner wives in the sample renders comparisons between significant effects obtained for the two sexes strictly nonequivalent. The addition of new work schedule characteristics (e.g., second job holding) to the list of predictors in the regression makes the test of each such characteristic more conservative. Likewise, the analysis of cross-over effects adds the work schedule characteristics of spouses to the predictor list, again making it more difficult for any one predictor to emerge as significant.

Methodological issues aside, a number of substantive findings also deserve comment although, unfortunately, lack of comparable published research precludes comparisons with existing data in all but a very few cases. In the first instance, within-couple similarity between the schedules of husbands and wives diminishes sex differences in schedules at the aggregate level; aggregate sex differences, nevertheless, do persist. Couples' joint schedule patterns prove instructive at the level of distributional data and they also prove related to selected demographic factors. Directly contrary to Robinson's (1977) bivariate data, the negative relationship in the present multivariate data between time in work and time in family roles emerges as stronger for women than for men. Several cross-over effects achieve statistical significance, meaning that a spouse's work schedule appears to have a bearing on a respondent's family life. Nevertheless, the family life of a member of a dual-earner couple seems much more strongly affected by his or her own work schedule than by that of his or her spouse. The latter finding conforms to common sense expectations. In addition, some of the cross-over effects that emerge make eminent sense. Wives' schedule conflicts, for example, respond to their husbands' engaging in regular weekend work, presumably because husbands who work on weekends reduce their time in child care and housework.

Implications of Our Findings for Future Research and Policy Making

If the issues raised by this report on work schedules and family life are already timely, all indications are that they will become increasingly salient in the future. As more women (especially married women) enter the labor force, the overall distribution of work schedules will change because women typically have different types of schedules from those reported by men. The influx of women will also draw greater attention to the circumstances of the two-earner couple and the special issues raised by having two jobs in one family. In addition, any trend toward less sex-typing of occupations will mean that men and women are engaged in more similar types of work and hence are likely to have more similar types of job schedules. Such a move away from stringent occupational sex typing implies smaller differences in the future between the job schedules of members of dual-earner couples. In view of the continuing importance of the relationship between work schedules and family life, this report concludes with a review of the implications of the present findings for future research and relevant policy decisions.

The imperfections and limitations of any research program inevitably point to profitable lines of future research; our study represents no exception. Already mentioned is the need for statistical procedures that take into account more complicated (e.g., bidirectional) causal patterns. Our analysis would also benefit from the inclusion of certain additional variables, some of which exist in or could be derived from the current dataset. A general attempt to develop multiple measures of the major concepts, wherever possible, would facilitate the use of more advanced causal modeling techniques. From a broader perspective, there remains the possibility of studying work schedules in conjunction with other dimensions of the job that also have implications for family life (e.g., income, measures of work performance, worker's level of absorption in the job, and job content), thereby addressing the larger issue of whether work schedules are among the more potent work-related influences on family life. There is, likewise, the possibility of investigating additional dimensions of family life such as decision-making power. A related and promising elaboration would be a joint examination of leisure and family activities. The two categories overlap considerably and information about each would add to understanding about the other. Some of our unanticipated findings about shiftwork, for example, might come into clearer focus if patterns of leisure and family activities were explored simultaneously.

Analyses of the sample of dual-earner couples would be enhanced by introducing and exploring measures of schedule control since such control, if available to one or both partners, might well provide some relief from the problems of juggling two work schedules in conjunction with family responsibilities. Investigations of dual-earner couples would also benefit greatly from datasets with information on the family life as well as the work schedules of *both* spouses. The present dataset, by contrast, lacks systematic information on the spouse's family life. A spouse's work schedule can be reported by a worker more reliably than a spouse's family life; thus future researchers must collect data on family life from both spouses in dual-earner couples. Despite the expense of taking two interviews in each two-earner household, the resulting data would nonetheless permit powerful causal analyses of the intertwined effects of the two partners' work schedules on their respective experiences of family life.

Notably absent in the current sample are part-time workers who total fewer than twenty hours of paid employment per week. Studies of the relationships between their work schedule characteristics and family life raise an important question. Can we extrapolate in some linear fashion from the results for those working in the upper range of weekly hours (i.e., twenty and above) to the lower portion of the part-time range? Certainly, we should not assume that connections between work schedules and family life become wholly trivial for those who work the fewest hours. Future research, therefore, will be needed to resolve empirical questions about the relationships between work schedules and family life for various portions of the hours range for part-time workers.

Other lines of future research might take a totally different direction. As pointed out earlier, national samples have distinct limitations when interest is high in very special or innovative arrangements. Samples with high proportions of shiftworkers would generate analyses of appreciably greater statistical power and, undoubtedly, uncover more significant relationships between shiftwork and the quality of family life. The same holds true for those working other nonstandard schedules including weekend work and second jobs. To take the latter example, a sample of workers with second jobs would open up a variety of attractive analytic options. The phenomenon of second jobs proves curiously analogous to the case of the two-earner family. In both instances, the central issue raised is the separate and combined impact of two job schedules on the experience of family life. Researchable questions about second jobs thus include: Does the second job schedule have any impact on a person's family life when controlling for the effects of the first job schedule? If so, does the second job schedule have as much impact on family life as the first one? Do the dimensions of the second job schedule have the same type of impact on measures of family life as the corresponding dimensions of the first job schedule? Is the impact of one job schedule on family life moderated by the nature of the other job schedule? It therefore seems clear that samples of workers with schedules of special interest hold considerable potential for supplementing what can be learned from national samples. Accordingly, it scarcely needs emphasizing that only the judicious use of a variety of research designs, samples, and analysis strategies will round out our understanding of the impact of work schedules on family life.

We conclude this report by reiterating what was said in Chapter 1 about the two major policy implications of our findings. In the first place, policy makers would do well to exploit the considerable potential of schedule control for improving the quality of family life. Schedule control refers to at least partial control over a variety of features of work schedules; it goes well beyond the issue implicit in flextime schedules, that is, flexibility of the starting and ending times of a day's work. Our report emphasizes that, in addition to its main effects on family life, schedule control can moderate the relationship between stressful work schedule characteristics and family life. Second, we have learned that, in the case of dual-earner couples, a person's family life can be affected by his or her spouse's work schedule as well as by his or her own schedule. Thus, in the decisions of policy makers about work schedules, the schedules of husbands and wives in such families deserve joint consideration.

Appendix A

Interview Schedule for the 1977 Quality of Employment Survey (Sections A, B, and H only)

(205) A1. If you were free to go into any type of job you wanted, what would your choice be?

_____

_____

_____

| 1. SAME AS R HAS NOW | 3. R WOULD WANT TO RETIRE OR NOT WORK | 5. R SPECIFIES SOME JOB OTHER THAN HIS/HER PRESENT ONE | 8. DON'T KNOW |

(10) A2. Now let's talk about your present job. What is your main occupation?

OCCUPATION: _____

A3. Can you tell me a little more about what you do?

_____

_____

_____

(12) A4. What kind of business or industry is that in?_____

_____

(9) A5. INTERVIEWER CHECK POINT; ASK IF NECESSARY

Are you self-employed, or do you work for someone else?

| 1. SELF-EMPLOYED | 5. WORKS FOR SOMEONE ELSE |

Attach this sheet to Page 1 of PINK self-employed form and continue with interview.

Attach this sheet to Page 1 of WHITE wage and salaried form and continue with interview.

REMEMBER TO CHECK APPROPRIATE BOX!

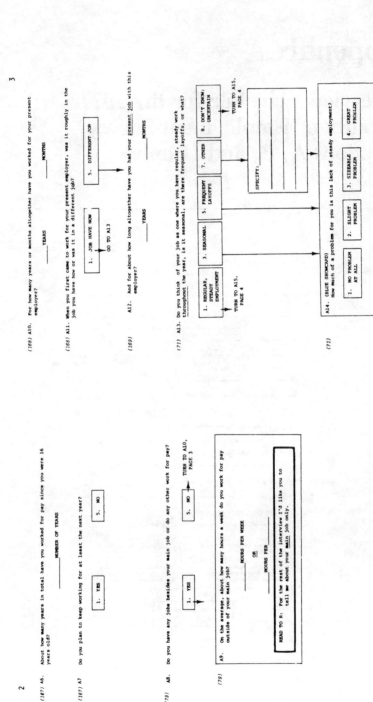

3

(168) A10. For how many years or months altogether have you worked for your present employer?
_____ YEARS   _____ MONTHS

(168) A11. When you first came to work for your present employer, was it roughly in the job you have now or was it in a different job?
1. JOB HAVE NOW → GO TO A13
5. DIFFERENT JOB

A12. And for about how long altogether have you had your present job with this employer?
(169)   _____ YEARS   _____ MONTHS

(71) A13. Do you think of your job as one where you have regular, steady work throughout the year, is it seasonal, are there frequent layoffs, or what?
1. REGULAR, STEADY EMPLOYMENT → TURN TO A15, PAGE 4
3. SEASONAL
5. FREQUENT LAYOFFS
7. OTHER
8. DON'T KNOW; UNCERTAIN → TURN TO A15, PAGE 4
SPECIFY: _____

(71) A14. (BLUE SHOWCARD) How much of a problem for you is this lack of steady employment?
1. NO PROBLEM AT ALL
2. SLIGHT PROBLEM
3. SIZEABLE PROBLEM
4. GREAT PROBLEM

2

(187) A6. About how many years in total have you worked for pay since you were 16 years old?
_____ NUMBER OF YEARS

(187) A7 Do you plan to keep working for at least the next year?
1. YES
5. NO

(79) A8. Do you have any jobs besides your main job or do any other work for pay?
1. YES
5. NO → TURN TO A10, PAGE 3

(79) A9. On the average, about how many hours a week do you work for pay outside of your main job?
_____ HOURS PER WEEK
OR
_____ HOURS PER _____

READ TO R: For the rest of the interview I'd like you to tell me about your main job only.

4

(78) A15. Were you laid off from your present job at any time in the last year?

1. YES →   5. NO → GO TO A19

(78) A16. How long were you laid off?

MONTHS ____   WEEKS ____   DAYS ____

(78) A17. (BLUE SHOWCARD)
How much of a problem for you (was/were) the layoff(s)?

1. NO PROBLEM AT ALL   2. SLIGHT PROBLEM   3. SIZEABLE PROBLEM   4. GREAT PROBLEM

(77) A18. Did you get any unemployment insurance benefits while you were laid off?

1. YES   5. NO

(9) A19. (RESPONDENT BOOKLET, PAGE 1)
About how many people work for your employer at the location where you work? I mean all types of workers in all areas and departments.

1. 1-9   2. 10-49   3. 50-99   4. 100-499
5. 500-999   6. 1000-1999   7. 2000 AND OVER   8. DON'T KNOW

(175) A20. How many people work for you and are paid by you. *(asked of self-employed only)*

NUMBER ____

A21. *THERE IS NO QUESTION A21.*

5

A22. (JOB DESCRIPTION--BLUE/YELLOW CARDS)
(194 unless otherwise noted)

There are many things people might say to describe their jobs. Some of them are written on this set of cards (HOLD UP CARDS). We would like to know whether or not these statements describe your job. Please put each yellow card below the blue card that best shows how much you agree or disagree with the statement.

(LAY DOWN BLUE ALTERNATIVE CARDS WITH "STRONGLY AGREE" ON R'S LEFT;
HAND YELLOW STATEMENT CARDS TO R TO SORT; COLLECT CARDS WITH BLUE CARDS ON
TOP OF EACH PILE, MARK ANY UNSORTED CARDS. RUBBER BAND THE CARDS, PLACE
THEM INSIDE THE BLUE ENVELOPE, AND RUBBER BAND THE ENVELOPE.)

CARDS IN THE ORDER IN WHICH THEY ARE GIVEN:

10. My job requires that I keep learning new things.
11. My job requires that I work very fast.
(243) 12. I have the freedom to decide what I do on my job.
13. My job requires a high level of skill.
(242) 14. What I do at work is more important to me than the money I earn.
15. My job requires that I work very hard.
(241) 16. A lot of people can be affected by how well I do my work.
17. It is basically my own responsibility to decide how my job gets done.
18. My job requires that I be creative.
19. I get to do a number of different things on my job.
20. I have a lot of say about what happens on my job.
21. My job lets me use my skills and abilities.
22. I decide when I take breaks.
23. On my job there are procedures for handling everything that comes up.
(239) 24. I decide who I work with on my job.
25. Most of the time I know what I have to do on my job.
(169) 26. My main satisfaction in life comes from my work.
27. It would be very hard for me to leave my job even if I wanted to.
28. I never seem to have enough time to get everything done on my job.
29. On my job, I can't satisfy everybody at the same time.
30. I determine the speed at which I work.
31. I have too much work to do everything well.
(169) 32. I am afraid of what might happen if I quit my job without having another one lined up.
(199) 33. The product or service I help provide is up to the standards that the public should get.
34. It is hard to tell what impact my work makes on the product or service.
35. To satisfy some people on my job, I have to upset others.
(242) 36. My main interest in my work is to get enough money to do the other things I want to do.
37. The work I do on my job is meaningful to me.
(277) 38. I have a lot of energy left over when I get off work.
39. On my job, I produce a whole product or perform a complete service.
40. On my job, I know exactly what is expected of me.
41. I feel that most of the things I do on my job are meaningless.
42. My job requires that I do the same things over and over.
43. Even if no one tells me, I can figure out how well I am doing on my job.
(169) 44. I feel personally responsible for the work I do on my job.
(240) 45. I have too much at stake in my job to change jobs now.
46. I'd be happier if I didn't have to work at all.
47. My job involves doing only a small part in producing the product or service.
48. I deserve all the credit or blame for how well I am doing in my work.
49. Supervisors or co-workers usually let me know how well I am doing in my work.
(190) 50. On my job, I have to do some things that go against my conscience.
51. My job has rules and regulations concerning almost everything I might do or say.

6

(241) A23. Altogether, how much effort, either physical or mental, does your job require--a lot, some, only a little, or none?

| 4. A LOT | 3. SOME | 2. ONLY A LITTLE | 1. NONE |

(242) A24. And how much effort do you put into your job beyond what is required-- a lot, some, only a little, or none?

| 4. A LOT | 3. SOME | 2. ONLY A LITTLE | 1. NONE |

(243) A25. On most days on your job, how often does time seem to drag for you--often, sometimes, rarely, or never?

| 1. OFTEN | 2. SOMETIMES | 3. RARELY | 4. NEVER |

(244/ 245) A26. How often do you think about your job when you're busy doing something else-- often, sometimes, rarely, or never?

| 1. OFTEN | 2. SOMETIMES | 3. RARELY | 4. NEVER |

(193) A27. (RESPONDENT BOOKLET, PAGE 2)
Suppose there were some particular duties on your job that you wanted changed. How hard would it be to get them changed?

| 4. VERY HARD | 3. SOMEWHAT HARD | 2. NOT TOO HARD | 1. NOT AT ALL HARD |

7

(201) A28. How useful and valuable will your present job skills be five years from now? Will they be very useful and valuable, somewhat, a little, or not at all useful and valuable?

| 4. VERY USEFUL & VALUABLE | 3. SOMEWHAT USEFUL & VALUABLE | 2. A LITTLE USEFUL & VALUABLE | 1. NOT AT ALL USEFUL & VALUABLE |

(202) A29. Do you have some skills from your experience and training that you would like to be using in your work but can't use on your present job?

| 1. YES | 5. NO |

(202) A30. What level of formal education do you feel is needed by a person in your job?

☐ 00 NONE
☐ 10 GRADES 1-7 (SOME GRADE SCHOOL)
☐ 20 GRADE 8 (COMPLETION OF GRADE SCHOOL)
☐ 30 GRADES 9-11 (SOME HIGH SCHOOL)
☐ 40 GRADE 12 (HIGH SCHOOL DIPLOMA, GED, OR ANY HIGH SCHOOL EQUIVALENT)
☐ 50 SOME COLLEGE WITHOUT DEGREE
☐ 51 SOME COLLEGE WITH DEGREE (GRADUATE OF JUNIOR COLLEGE)
☐ 60 GRADE 16 (COLLEGE DEGREE)
☐ 70 GRADUATE OR PROFESSIONAL EDUCATION IN EXCESS OF COLLEGE DEGREE

(203) A31. How long would it take the average person with that much education to learn to do your job reasonably well?

_____ YEARS _____ MONTHS _____ WEEKS _____ DAYS

| RIGHT AWAY, NO TIME AT ALL |

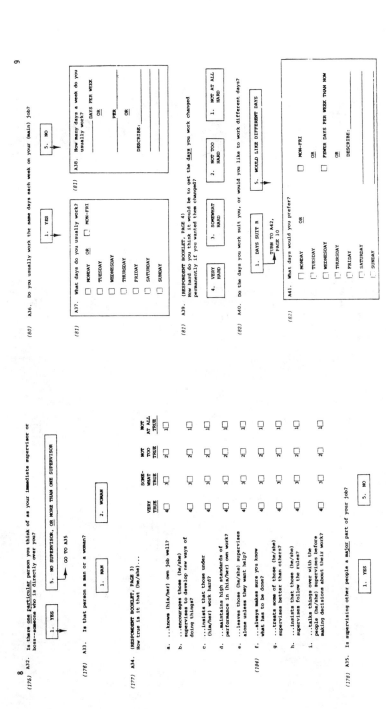

8

(175) A32. Is there **one particular** person you think of as your immediate supervisor or boss--someone who is directly over you?

1. YES

5. NO SUPERVISOR, OR MORE THAN ONE SUPERVISOR → GO TO A35

(176) A33. Is that person a man or a woman?

1. MAN   2. WOMAN

(177) A34. (RESPONDENT BOOKLET, PAGE 3)
How true is it that (he/she)...

	VERY TRUE	SOMEWHAT TRUE	NOT TOO TRUE	NOT AT ALL TRUE
a. ...knows (his/her) own job well?	4	3	2	1
b. ...encourages those (he/she) supervises to develop new ways of doing things?	4	3	2	1
c. ...insists that those under (his/her) work hard?	4	3	2	1
d. ...maintains high standards of performance in (his/her) own work?	4	3	2	1
e. ...leaves those (he/she) supervises alone unless they want help?	4	3	2	1
f. ...always makes sure you know what has to be done?	4	3	2	1
g. ...treats some of those (he/she) supervises better than others?	4	3	2	1
h. ...insists that those (he/she) supervises follow the rules?	4	3	2	1
i. ...talks things over with the people (he/she) supervises before making decisions about their work?	4	3	2	1

(184) [for f/g?]

(178) A35. Is supervising other people a **major** part of your job?

1. YES   5. NO

9

(180) A36. Do you usually work the same days each week on your (main) job?

1. YES   5. NO

(181) A37. What days do you usually work?

MONDAY OR MON-FRI
TUESDAY
WEDNESDAY
THURSDAY
FRIDAY
SATURDAY
SUNDAY

(81) A38. How many days a week do you usually work?

____ DAYS PER WEEK
OR
____ PER
OR
DESCRIBE:

(81) A39. (RESPONDENT BOOKLET, PAGE 4)
How hard do you think it would be to get the days you work changed permanently if you wanted them changed?

4. VERY HARD   3. SOMEWHAT HARD   2. NOT TOO HARD   1. NOT AT ALL HARD

(82) A40. Do the days you work suit you, or would you like to work different days?

1. DAYS SUIT R → TURN TO A42, PAGE 10

5. WOULD LIKE DIFFERENT DAYS

(82) A41. What days would you prefer?

MONDAY OR MON-FRI
TUESDAY
WEDNESDAY
THURSDAY
FRIDAY FEWER DAYS PER WEEK THAN NOW
SATURDAY OR
SUNDAY DESCRIBE:

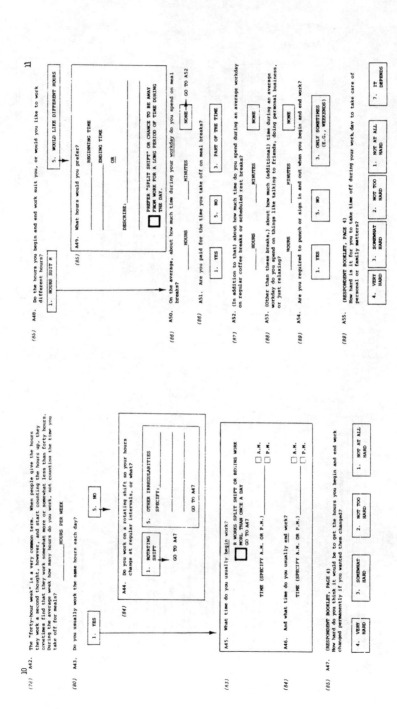

10

(72) A42. The "forty-hour week" is a very common term. When people give the hours they work a second thought, however, and start counting the hours up, they sometimes find that they work somewhat more or somewhat less than forty hours. During the average week how many hours do you work, not counting the time you take off for meals?
_____ HOURS PER WEEK

(80) A43. Do you usually work the same hours each day?
1. YES
5. NO

(84) A44. Do you work on a rotating shift so your hours change at regular intervals, or what?
1. ROTATING SHIFT → GO TO A47
5. OTHER IRREGULARITIES SPECIFY: _____ GO TO A47

(83) A45. What time do you usually begin work?
[ ] R WORKS SPLIT SHIFT OR BEGINS WORK MORE THAN ONCE A DAY → GO TO A47
TIME (SPECIFY A.M. OR P.M.) _____ □ A.M. □ P.M.

(84) A46. And what time do you usually end work?
TIME (SPECIFY A.M. OR P.M.) _____ □ A.M. □ P.M.

(85) A47. (RESPONDENT BOOKLET, PAGE 4)
How hard do you think it would be to get the hours you begin and end work changed permanently if you wanted them changed?
4. VERY HARD
3. SOMEWHAT HARD
2. NOT TOO HARD
1. NOT AT ALL HARD

11

(85) A48. Do the hours you begin and end work suit you, or would you like to work different hours?
1. HOURS SUIT R
5. WOULD LIKE DIFFERENT HOURS

(85) A49. What hours would you prefer?
BEGINNING TIME _____
ENDING TIME _____
OR
DESCRIBE: _____
[ ] PREFER "SPLIT SHIFT" OR CHANCE TO BE AWAY FROM WORK FOR A LONG PERIOD OF TIME DURING THE DAY.

(86) A50. On the average, about how much time during your workday do you spend on meal breaks?
_____ HOURS _____ MINUTES NONE → GO TO A52

(86) A51. Are you paid for the time you take off on meal breaks?
1. YES
5. NO
3. PART OF THE TIME

(87) A52. (In addition to that) about how much time do you spend during an average workday on regular coffee breaks or scheduled rest breaks?
_____ HOURS _____ MINUTES NONE

(88) A53. (Other than these breaks,) about how much (additional) time during an average workday do you spend on things like talking to friends, doing personal business, or just relaxing?
_____ HOURS _____ MINUTES NONE

(89) A54. Are you required to punch or sign in and out when you begin and end work?
1. YES
5. NO
3. ONLY SOMETIMES (E.G., WEEKENDS)

(89) A55. (RESPONDENT BOOKLET, PAGE 4)
How hard is it for you to take time off during your work day to take care of personal or family matters?
4. VERY HARD
3. SOMEWHAT HARD
2. NOT TOO HARD
1. NOT AT ALL HARD
7. IT DEPENDS

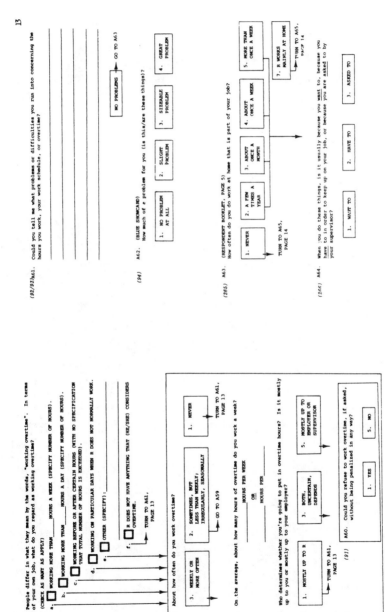

12

(88) A56. People differ in what they mean by the words, "working overtime". In terms of your own job, what do you regard as working overtime? (CHECK AS MANY AS APPLY)

- a. ☐ WORKING MORE THAN ___ HOURS A WEEK (SPECIFY NUMBER OF HOURS).
- b. ☐ WORKING MORE THAN ___ HOURS A DAY (SPECIFY NUMBER OF HOURS).
- c. ☐ WORKING BEFORE OR AFTER CERTAIN HOURS (WITH NO SPECIFICATION THAT TOTAL NUMBER OF HOURS IS EXCEEDED).
- d. ☐ WORKING ON PARTICULAR DAYS WHEN R DOES NOT NORMALLY WORK.
- e. ☐ OTHER (SPECIFY): ___
- f. ☐ R DOES NOT HAVE ANYTHING THAT (HE/SHE) CONSIDERS OVERTIME.
  TURN TO A61, PAGE 13

(90) A57. About how often do you work overtime?

- 3. WEEKLY OR MORE OFTEN
- 2. SOMETIMES, BUT LESS THAN WEEKLY; IRREGULARLY, SEASONALLY → GO TO A59
- 1. NEVER → TURN TO A61, PAGE 13

(90) A58. On the average, about how many hours of overtime do you work a week?

___ HOURS PER WEEK

OR

___ HOURS PER ___

(91) A59. Who determines whether you're going to put in overtime hours? Is it mostly up to you or mostly up to your employer?

- 1. MOSTLY UP TO R → TURN TO A61, PAGE 13
- 3. BOTH, UNCERTAIN, DEPENDS
- 5. MOSTLY UP TO EMPLOYER OR SUPERVISOR

(91) A60. Could you refuse to work overtime, if asked, without being penalized in any way?

- 1. YES
- 5. NO

13

(92/93) A61. Could you tell me what problems or difficulties you run into concerning the hours you work, your work schedule, or overtime?

___

___

___

NO PROBLEMS → GO TO A63

(94) A62. (BLUE SHOWCARD) How much of a problem for you (is this/are these things)?

- 1. NO PROBLEM AT ALL
- 2. SLIGHT PROBLEM
- 3. SIZEABLE PROBLEM
- 4. GREAT PROBLEM

(265) A63. (RESPONDENT BOOKLET, PAGE 5) How often do you do work at home that is part of your job?

- 1. NEVER → TURN TO A65, PAGE 14
- 2. A FEW TIMES A YEAR
- 3. ABOUT ONCE A MONTH
- 4. ABOUT ONCE A WEEK
- 5. MORE THAN ONCE A WEEK
- 7. R WORKS MAINLY AT HOME → TURN TO A65, PAGE 14

(266) A64. When you do these things, is it usually because you want to, because you have to in order to keep up on your job, or because you are asked to by your supervisor?

- 1. WANT TO
- 2. HAVE TO
- 3. ASKED TO

15

SECTION B

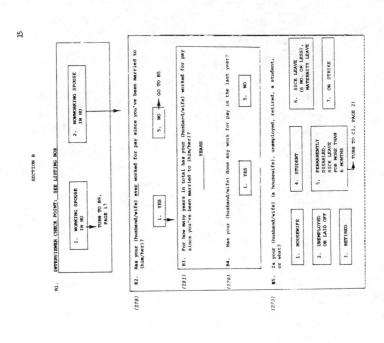

B1. INTERVIEWER CHECK POINT: SEE LISTING BOX

1. WORKING SPOUSE IN HU — TURN TO B9, PAGE 17

2. NONWORKING SPOUSE IN HU

(279) B2. Has your (husband/wife) *ever* worked for pay since you've been married to (him/her)?

1. YES

5. NO → GO TO B5

(281) B3. For how many years in total has your (husband/wife) worked for pay since you've been married to (him/her)? _____ YEARS

(279) B4. Has your (husband/wife) done any work for pay in the last year?

1. YES

5. NO

(273) B5. Is your (husband/wife) (a housewife), unemployed, retired, a student, or what?

1. HOUSEWIFE
2. UNEMPLOYED OR LAID OFF
3. RETIRED
4. STUDENT
5. PERMANENTLY DISABLED, SICK LEAVE FOR MORE THAN 6 MONTHS — TURN TO C1, PAGE 21
6. SICK LEAVE (6 MO. OR LESS), MATERNITY LEAVE
7. ON STRIKE

14

A65. INTERVIEWER CHECK POINT: SEE LISTING BOX ON COVER SHEET

1. R HAS ANY FAMILY MEMBERS 14 OR OVER IN HU

5. R DOES NOT HAVE ANY FAMILY MEMBERS 14 OR OVER IN HU — GO TO A67

(286) A66. (RESPONDENT BOOKLET, PAGE 5) How often do family members in your household help you with or do things that are part of your job?

5. MORE THAN ONCE A WEEK
4. ABOUT ONCE A WEEK
3. ABOUT ONCE A MONTH
2. A FEW TIMES A YEAR
1. NEVER

(261) A67. On the average, on days when you're working, about how much time do you spend on home chores—things like cooking, cleaning, repairs, shopping, yardwork, and keeping track of money and bills? _____ HOURS PER DAY

(260) A68. And about how much time on days when you're *not* working? _____ HOURS PER DAY

A69. INTERVIEWER CHECK POINT: SEE LISTING BOX

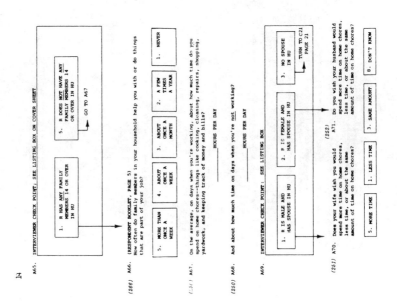

1. R IS MALE AND HAS SPOUSE IN HU

2. R IS FEMALE AND HAS SPOUSE IN HU

3. NO SPOUSE IN HU — TURN TO C21 PAGE 21

(261) A70. Does your wife wish you would spend more time on home chores, less time, or about the same amount of time on home chores?

(262) A71. Do you wish your husband would spend more time on home chores, less time, or about the same amount of time on home chores?

5. MORE TIME
1. LESS TIME
3. SAME AMOUNT
8. DON'T KNOW

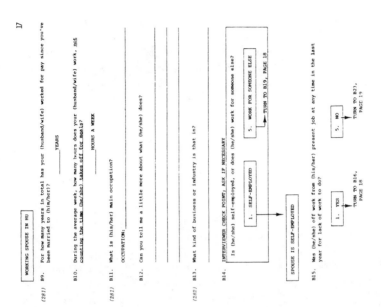

17

WORKING SPOUSE IN HU

(281) B9. For how many years in total has your (husband/wife) worked for pay since you've been married to (him/her)?

___ YEARS

B10. During the average week, how many hours does your (husband/wife) work, not counting the time (he/she) takes off for meals?

___ HOURS A WEEK

(281) B11. What is (his/her) main occupation?

OCCUPATION: ___

B12. Can you tell me a little more about what (he/she) does?

_____

_____

(282) B13. What kind of business or industry is that in?

B14. INTERVIEWER CHECK POINT; ASK IF NECESSARY

Is (he/she) self-employed, or does (he/she) work for someone else?

1. SELF-EMPLOYED   5. WORK FOR SOMEONE ELSE
→ TURN TO B19, PAGE 18

SPOUSE IS SELF-EMPLOYED

B15. Was (he/she) off work from (his/her) present job at any time in the last year for lack of work to do?

1. YES
TURN TO B16, PAGE 18

5. NO
TURN TO B23, PAGE 19

16

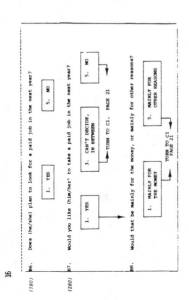

(280) B6. Does (he/she) plan to look for a paid job in the next year?

1. YES   5. NO

(280) B7. Would you like (him/her) to take a paid job in the next year?

1. YES   3. CAN'T DECIDE, IN BETWEEN   5. NO
→ TURN TO C1, PAGE 21

B8. Would that be mainly for the money, or mainly for other reasons?

1. MAINLY FOR THE MONEY   5. MAINLY FOR OTHER REASONS
TURN TO C1 PAGE 21

Data for questions B8, B10, B12, B14-B19, B28, and B34 are not included in this volume.

19

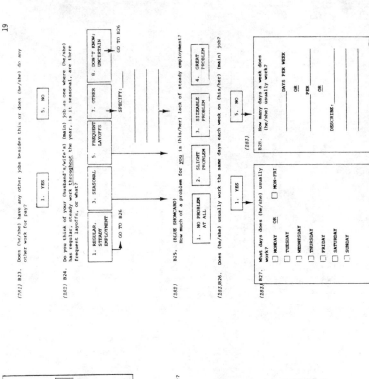

(281) B23. Does (he/she) have any other jobs besides this or does (he/she) do any other work for pay?

1. YES   5. NO

(282) B24. Do you think of your (husband's/wife's) (main) job as one where (he/she) has regular, steady work throughout the year, is it seasonal, are there frequent layoffs, or what?

1. REGULAR, STEADY EMPLOYMENT → GO TO B26
3. SEASONAL
5. FREQUENT LAYOFFS
7. OTHER   SPECIFY: _____
8. DON'T KNOW; UNCERTAIN → GO TO B26

(282) B25. (BLUE SHOWCARD) How much of a problem for you is (his/her) lack of steady employment?

1. NO PROBLEM AT ALL 2. SLIGHT PROBLEM 3. SIZEABLE PROBLEM 4. GREAT PROBLEM

(283)/B26. Does (he/she) usually work the same days each week on (his/her) (main) job?

1. YES   5. NO

(283) B27. What days does (he/she) usually work?

MONDAY OR ☐ MON-FRI
☐ TUESDAY
☐ WEDNESDAY
☐ THURSDAY
☐ FRIDAY
☐ SATURDAY
☐ SUNDAY

(283) B28. How many days a week does (he/she) usually work?

_____ DAYS PER WEEK
OR _____ PER
OR
DESCRIBE: _____

18

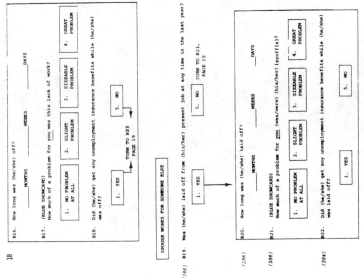

B16. How long was (he/she) off?

_____ MONTHS _____ WEEKS _____ DAYS

B17. (BLUE SHOWCARD) How much of a problem for you was this lack of work?

1. NO PROBLEM AT ALL 2. SLIGHT PROBLEM 3. SIZEABLE PROBLEM 4. GREAT PROBLEM

B18. Did (he/she) get any unemployment insurance benefits while (he/she) was off?

1. YES   5. NO → TURN TO B23, PAGE 19

SPOUSE WORKS FOR SOMEONE ELSE

(286) B19. Was (he/she) laid off from (his/her) present job at any time in the last year?

1. YES   5. NO → TURN TO B23, PAGE 19

(286) B20. How long was (he/she) laid off?

_____ MONTHS _____ WEEKS _____ DAYS

(286) B21. (BLUE SHOWCARD) How much of a problem for you (was/were) (his/her) layoff(s)?

1. NO PROBLEM AT ALL 2. SLIGHT PROBLEM 3. SIZEABLE PROBLEM 4. GREAT PROBLEM

(284) B22. Did (he/she) get any unemployment insurance benefits while (he/she) was laid off?

1. YES   5. NO

20

(303) B29. Does (he/she) usually work the same hours each day?

1. YES →

5. NO → GO TO B32

(283) B30. What time does (he/she) usually begin work?

☐ SPOUSE WORKS SPLIT SHIFT OR BEGINS WORK MORE THAN ONCE A DAY GO TO B32

OR

TIME (SPECIFY A.M. OR P.M.) _____   ☐ A.M.   ☐ P.M.

(286) B31. And what time does (he/she) usually end work?

TIME (SPECIFY A.M. OR P.M.) _____   ☐ A.M.   ☐ P.M.

(280) B32. Does your (husband/wife) plan to keep working for at least the next year?

1. YES

5. NO

(280) B33. Would you like (him/her) to keep working for at least the next year?

1. YES →

5. NO → TURN TO CL. PAGE 21

B34. Would that be mainly for the money, or mainly for other reasons?

1. MAINLY FOR THE MONEY

5. MAINLY FOR OTHER REASONS

60

SECTION H

(57) H1. Which would you rather have on your present job . . . a 10% pay raise . . .

	10% PAY RAISE	OTHER IMPROVEMENT	DON'T KNOW CAN'T DECIDE
a. . . .or more job security?	1. $	5. SECURITY	8
b. . . .or less tiring work (physical or mental)?	1. $	5. LESS TIRING	8
c. . . .or a little safer or healthier working conditions?	1. $	5. SAFER	8
d. . . .or a more comfortable and pleasant work place?	1. $	5. COMFORTABLE	8
e. . . .or more interesting work?	1. $	5. INTERESTING	8
f. . . .or more freedom to decide how to do your work?	1. $	5. FREEDOM	8
g. . . .or more paid vacation days?	1. $	5. VACATION	8
h. . . .or better retirement benefits?	1. $	5. RETIREMENT	0
j. . . .or better medical insurance benefits?	1. $	5. MEDICAL	0
k. . . .or a better chance for promotion?	1. $	5. PROMOTION	0
m. . . .or a shorter work week— that is, fewer hours per week?	1. $	5. SHORTER HOURS	0

61

(173) H2. (RESPONDENT BOOKLET, PAGE 15)
Suppose you were offered a job that is much better than your present one, but located in another community at least 100 miles away. How willing would you be to move to the other community to take the better job?

4. VERY WILLING	3. SOMEWHAT WILLING	2. NOT TOO WILLING	1. NOT AT ALL WILLING	7. DEPENDS ON CIRCUMSTANCES (SPECIFY)

GO TO H4

(173) H3. Why wouldn't you be willing to move?

_____
_____
_____

(173) H4. (RESPONDENT BOOKLET, PAGE 15)
Suppose you were out of work and couldn't find a job near where you live but were offered a steady job somewhere else. How willing would you be to move to a community at least 100 miles away to take the job?

4. VERY WILLING	3. SOMEWHAT WILLING	2. NOT TOO WILLING	1. NOT AT ALL WILLING	7. DEPENDS ON CIRCUMSTANCES (SPECIFY)

TURN TO H6,
PAGE 62

(173) H5. Why wouldn't you be willing to move?
☐ SAME REASON AS GIVEN IN H3

_____
_____
_____

62

(170) H6. Is there a shortage of workers in this (geographical) area who have your experience, training, and skills?

☐ 1. YES   ☐ 5. NO   ☐ 8. DON'T KNOW
  GO TO H8

(1721) H7. Would you say there's a shortage of jobs in this (geographical) area for people with your experience, training, and skills?

☐ 1. YES   ☐ 5. NO   ☐ 8. DON'T KNOW

(170) H8. About how easy would it be for you to find a job with another employer with approximately the same income and fringe benefits you now have? Would you say very very easy, somewhat easy, or not easy at all?

☐ 5. VERY EASY   ☐ 3. SOMEWHAT EASY   ☐ 1. NOT EASY AT ALL

(1721) H9. (RESPONDENT BOOKLET, PAGE 16)
Sometimes people permanently lose jobs they want to keep. How likely is it that during the next couple of years you will lose your present job and have to look for a job with another employer?

☐ 4. VERY LIKELY   ☐ 3. SOMEWHAT LIKELY   ☐ 2. NOT TOO LIKELY   ☐ 1. NOT AT ALL LIKELY   ☐ 7. INAPPROPRIATE (E.G., RETIRING, QUITTING)
                                        TURN TO H11, PAGE 63

(1722) H10. Why might this happen?

_____
_____
_____
_____
_____

63

(247) H11. INTERVIEWER CHECK POINT; SEE LISTING BOX

☐ 1. SPOUSE IN HU   ☐ NO SPOUSE IN HU
   TURN TO H19,
   PAGE 65

Now, for a few background questions. Are you married, widowed, separated, divorced, have you never been married, or what?

☐ 2. WIDOWED   ☐ 3. SEPARATED   ☐ 4. DIVORCED

☐ 5. NEVER MARRIED   ☐ 6. MARRIED BUT SPOUSE NOT IN HU   ☐ 7. LIVING TOGETHER, COMMON-LAW MARRIAGE

(8) H12. When were you born?

_____   _____   _____
MONTH   DAY   YEAR

(8) H13. What is the highest grade of school or level of education you completed?

☐ 00 NONE
☐ 10 GRADES 1-7 (SOME GRADE SCHOOL)
☐ 20 GRADE 8 (COMPLETION OF GRADE SCHOOL)
☐ 30 GRADES 9-11 (SOME HIGH SCHOOL)
☐ 40 GRADE 12 (HIGH SCHOOL DIPLOMA, GED, OR ANY HIGH SCHOOL EQUIVALENT)
☐ 50 SOME COLLEGE WITHOUT DEGREE
☐ 51 SOME COLLEGE WITH DEGREE (GRADUATE OF JUNIOR COLLEGE)
☐ 60 GRADE 16 (COLLEGE DEGREE)
☐ 70 GRADUATE OR PROFESSIONAL EDUCATION IN EXCESS OF COLLEGE DEGREE

65

MARRIED R's, SPOUSE IN HU

(8) H19. Now, for a few background questions. When were you born?

MONTH _____   DAY _____   YEAR _____

(8) H20. What is the highest grade of school or level of education you completed?

- [ ] 00 NONE
- [ ] 10 GRADES 1-7 (SOME GRADE SCHOOL)
- [ ] 20 GRADE 8 (COMPLETION OF GRADE SCHOOL)
- [ ] 30 GRADES 9-11 (SOME HIGH SCHOOL)
- [ ] 40 GRADE 12 (HIGH SCHOOL DIPLOMA, GED, OR ANY HIGH SCHOOL EQUIVALENT)
- [ ] 50 SOME COLLEGE WITHOUT DEGREE
- [ ] 51 SOME COLLEGE WITH DEGREE (GRADUATE OF JUNIOR COLLEGE)
- [ ] 60 GRADE 16 (COLLEGE DEGREE)
- [ ] 70 GRADUATE OR PROFESSIONAL EDUCATION IN EXCESS OF COLLEGE DEGREE

(203) H21. Have you ever gone to a trade school?

1. YES →

5. NO → TURN TO H23, PAGE 66

(203) H22. How many years of trade school did you complete?

_____ YEARS

64

(203) H14. Have you ever gone to a trade school?

1. YES →

5. NO → GO TO H16

(203) H15. How many years of trade school did you complete?

_____ YEARS

(249) H16. How many dependents do you have, that is, others who depend on you for their financial support?

_____ DEPENDENTS

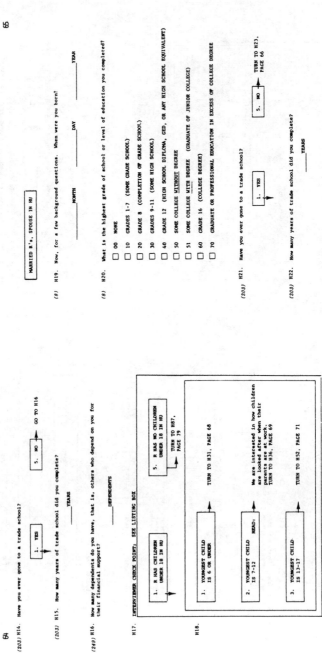

H17. INTERVIEWER CHECK POINT, SEE LISTING BOX

1. R HAS CHILDREN UNDER 18 IN HU →

5. R HAS NO CHILDREN UNDER 18 IN HU → TURN TO H97, PAGE 79

H18.

1. YOUNGEST CHILD IS 6 OR UNDER → TURN TO H31, PAGE 68

2. YOUNGEST CHILD IS 7-12 → READ: We are interested in how children are looked after when their parents are at work. TURN TO H36, PAGE 69

3. YOUNGEST CHILD IS 13-17 → TURN TO H52, PAGE 71

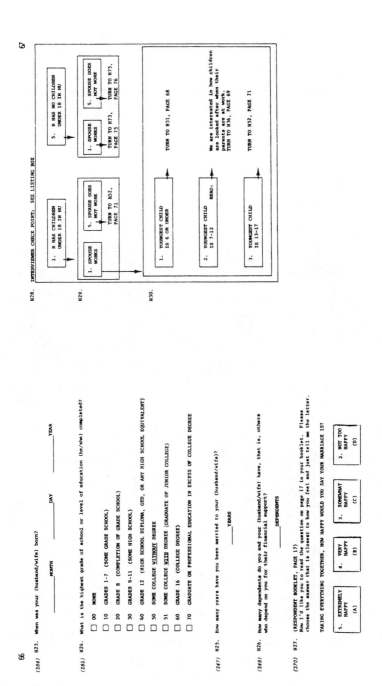

(284) H23. When was your (husband/wife) born?

_____   _____   _____
MONTH   DAY   YEAR

(285) H24. What is the highest grade of school or level of education (he/she) completed?

☐ 00 NONE

☐ 10 GRADES 1-7 (SOME GRADE SCHOOL)

☐ 20 GRADE 8 (COMPLETION OF GRADE SCHOOL)

☐ 30 GRADES 9-11 (SOME HIGH SCHOOL)

☐ 40 GRADE 12 (HIGH SCHOOL DIPLOMA, GED, OR ANY HIGH SCHOOL EQUIVALENT)

☐ 50 SOME COLLEGE WITHOUT DEGREE

☐ 51 SOME COLLEGE WITH DEGREE (GRADUATE OF JUNIOR COLLEGE)

☐ 60 GRADE 16 (COLLEGE DEGREE)

☐ 70 GRADUATE OR PROFESSIONAL EDUCATION IN EXCESS OF COLLEGE DEGREE

(247) H25. How many years have you been married to your (husband/wife)?

_____ YEARS

(249) H26. How many dependents do you and your (husband/wife) have, that is, others who depend on you for their financial support?

_____ DEPENDENTS

(320) H27. (RESPONDENT BOOKLET, PAGE 17)
Now I'd like you to read the question on page 17 in your booklet. Please choose the answer that is closest to how you feel and just tell me the letter.

TAKING EVERYTHING TOGETHER, HOW HAPPY WOULD YOU SAY YOUR MARRIAGE IS?

5. EXTREMELY HAPPY (A)	4. VERY HAPPY (B)	3. SOMEWHAT HAPPY (C)	2. NOT TOO HAPPY (D)

H28. INTERVIEWER CHECK POINT, SEE LISTING BOX

H29.

1. R HAS CHILDREN UNDER 18 IN HU

| 1. SPOUSE WORKS | 5. SPOUSE DOES NOT WORK TURN TO H52, PAGE 71 |

5. R HAS NO CHILDREN UNDER 18 IN HU

| 1. SPOUSE WORKS TURN TO H73, PAGE 75 | 5. SPOUSE DOES NOT WORK TURN TO H75, PAGE 76 |

H30.

We are interested in how children are looked after when their parents are at work.
TURN TO H36, PAGE 69

1. YOUNGEST CHILD IS 6 OR UNDER   →   TURN TO H31, PAGE 68

2. YOUNGEST CHILD IS 7-12   READ: →

3. YOUNGEST CHILD IS 13-17   →   TURN TO H52, PAGE 71

67

66

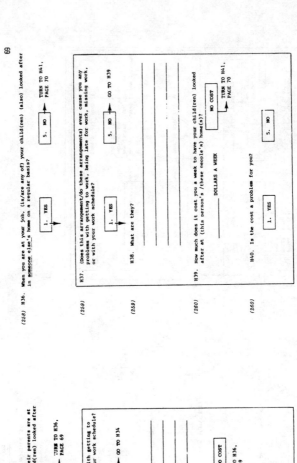

68

(258) H31. We are interested in how children are looked after when their parents are at work. When you are at your job, (is/are any of) your child(ren) looked after at a day care center or nursery school on a regular basis?

1. YES →

5. NO → TURN TO H36, PAGE 69

(259) H32. Do these arrangements ever cause you any problems with getting to work, being late for work, missing work, or with your work schedule?

1. YES →

5. NO → GO TO H34

(259) H33. What are they?

_____
_____
_____

(260) H34. How much do these arrangements cost you a week?

_____ DOLLARS A WEEK

NO COST → TURN TO H36, PAGE 69

(260) H35. Is the cost a problem for you?

1. YES

5. NO

69

(258) H36. When you are at your job, (is/are any of) your child(ren) (also) looked after in someone else's home on a regular basis?

1. YES →

5. NO → TURN TO H41, PAGE 70

(259) H37. (Does this arrangement/do these arrangements) ever cause you any problems with getting to work, being late for work, missing work, or with your work schedule?

1. YES →

5. NO → GO TO H39

(259) H38. What are they?

_____
_____
_____

(260) H39. How much does it cost you a week to have your child(ren) looked after at (this person's/these people's) home(s)?

_____ DOLLARS A WEEK

NO COST → TURN TO H41, PAGE 70

(260) H40. Is the cost a problem for you?

1. YES

5. NO

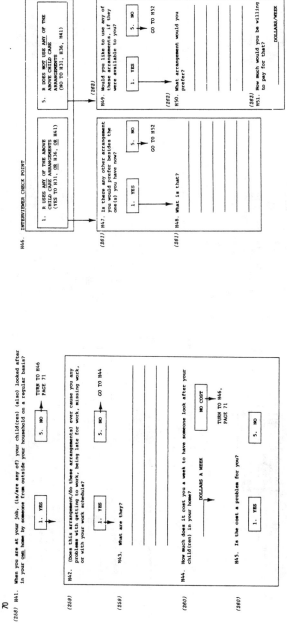

70

(258) H41. When you are at your job, (is/are any of) your child(ren) (also) looked after in your own home by someone from outside your household on a regular basis?

1. YES   5. NO → TURN TO H46 PAGE 71

(259) H42. (Does this arrangement/do these arrangements) ever cause you any problems with getting to work, being late for work, missing work, or with your work schedule?

1. YES   5. NO → GO TO H44

(259) H43. What are they?

_____

(260) H44. How much does it cost you a week to have someone look after your child(ren) in your home?

_____ DOLLARS A WEEK   NO COST → TURN TO H46, PAGE 71

(260) H45. Is the cost a problem for you?

1. YES   5. NO

71

H46. INTERVIEWER CHECK POINT

1. R USES ANY OF THE ABOVE CHILD CARE ARRANGEMENTS (YES TO H31, OR H36, OR H41)

5. R DOES NOT USE ANY OF THE ABOVE CHILD CARE ARRANGEMENTS (NO TO H31, H36, H41)

(261) H47. Is there any other arrangement you would prefer besides the one(s) you have now?

1. YES   5. NO → GO TO H52

(261) H48. What is that?

_____

(262) H49. Would you like to use any of these arrangements, if they were available to you?

1. YES   5. NO → GO TO H52

(262) H50. What arrangement would you prefer?

_____

(263) H51. How much would you be willing to pay for that?

_____ DOLLARS/WEEK

(253) H52. On the average, on days when you're working, about how much time do you spend (taking care of or) doing things with your child(ren)?

_____ HOURS PER DAY

(253) H53. And how much time on days when you're not working?

_____ HOURS PER DAY

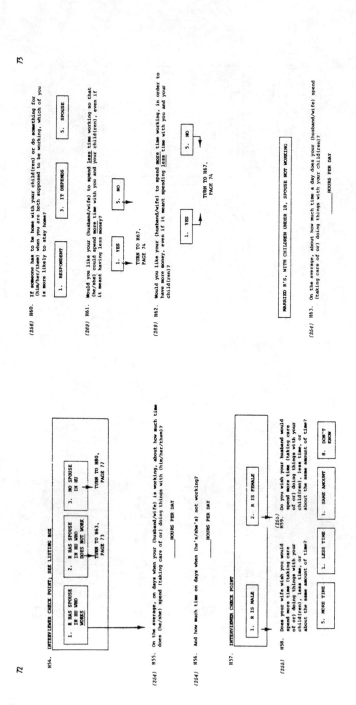

72

H54. INTERVIEWER CHECK POINT, SEE LISTING BOX

1. R HAS SPOUSE IN HU WHO WORKS

2. R HAS SPOUSE IN HU WHO DOES NOT WORK → TURN TO H63, PAGE 73

3. NO SPOUSE IN HU → TURN TO H80, PAGE 77

(254) H55. On the average, on days when your (husband/wife) is working, about how much time does (he/she) spend (taking care of or) doing things with (him/her/them)?

____ HOURS PER DAY

(254) H56. And how much time on days when (he's/she's) not working?

____ HOURS PER DAY

H57. INTERVIEWER CHECK POINT

1. R IS MALE

2. R IS FEMALE

(255) H58. Does your wife wish you would spend more time (taking care of or) doing things with your child(ren), less time, or about the same amount of time?

(255) H59. Do you wish your husband would spend more time (taking care of or) doing things with your child(ren), less time, or about the same amount of time?

5. MORE TIME | 1. LESS TIME | 3. SAME AMOUNT | 8. DON'T KNOW

73

(256) H60. If someone has to be home with your child(ren) or do something for (him/her/them) when you are both supposed to be working, which of you is more likely to stay home?

1. RESPONDENT | 3. IT DEPENDS | 5. SPOUSE

(289) H61. Would you like your (husband/wife) to spend less time working so that (he/she) could spend more time with you and your child(ren), even if it meant having less money?

1. YES — TURN TO H67, PAGE 74

5. NO

(289) H62. Would you like your (husband/wife) to spend more time working, in order to have more money, even if it meant spending less time with you and your child(ren)?

1. YES — TURN TO H67, PAGE 74

5. NO

MARRIED R'S, WITH CHILDREN UNDER 18, SPOUSE NOT WORKING

(254) H63. On the average, about how much time a day does your (husband/wife) spend (taking care of or) doing things with your child(ren)?

____ HOURS PER DAY

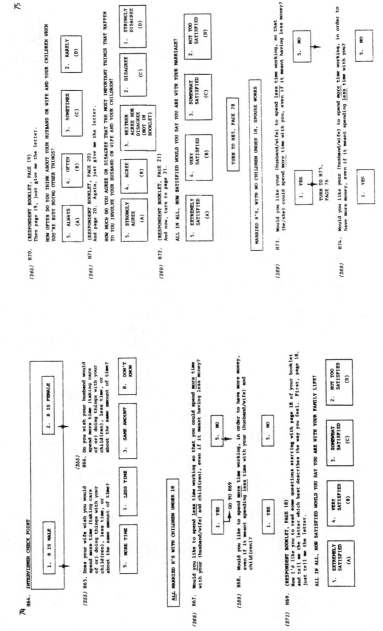

75

(245) H70. (RESPONDENT BOOKLET, PAGE 19)
Then page 19, just give me the letter.

HOW OFTEN DO YOU THINK ABOUT YOUR HUSBAND OR WIFE AND YOUR CHILDREN WHEN YOU'RE BUSY DOING OTHER THINGS?

5. ALWAYS (A) 4. OFTEN (B) 3. SOMETIMES (C) 2. RARELY (D)

(245) H71. (RESPONDENT BOOKLET, PAGE 20)
And page 20. Again, just give me the letter.

HOW MUCH DO YOU AGREE OR DISAGREE THAT THE MOST IMPORTANT THINGS THAT HAPPEN TO YOU INVOLVE YOUR HUSBAND OR WIFE AND YOUR CHILDREN?

5. STRONGLY AGREE (A) 4. AGREE (B) 3. NEITHER AGREE NOR DISAGREE (NOT IN BOOKLET) 2. DISAGREE (C) 1. STRONGLY DISAGREE (D)

(269) H72. (RESPONDENT BOOKLET, PAGE 21)
And now, turn to page 21.

ALL IN ALL, HOW SATISFIED WOULD YOU SAY YOU ARE WITH YOUR MARRIAGE?

5. EXTREMELY SATISFIED (A) 4. VERY SATISFIED (B) 3. SOMEWHAT SATISFIED (C) 2. NOT TOO SATISFIED (D)

TURN TO H85, PAGE 78

MARRIED R'S, WITH NO CHILDREN UNDER 18, SPOUSE WORKS

(269) H73. Would you like your (husband/wife) to spend less time working, so that (he/she) could spend more time with you, even if it meant having less money?

1. YES → TURN TO H77, PAGE 76   5. NO

(269) H74. Would you like your (husband/wife) to spend more time working, in order to have more money, even if it meant spending less time with you?

1. YES   5. NO

74

H64. INTERVIEWER CHECK POINT

1. R IS MALE   2. R IS FEMALE

(255) H65. Does your wife with you would spend more time (taking care of or) doing things with your child(ren), less time, or about the same amount of time?

(255) H66. Do you wish your husband would spend more time (taking care of or) doing things with your child(ren), less time, or about the same amount of time?

5. MORE TIME 1. LESS TIME 3. SAME AMOUNT 8. DON'T KNOW

ALL MARRIED R'S WITH CHILDREN UNDER 18

(268) H67. Would you like to spend less time working so that you could spend more time with your (husband/wife) and child(ren), even if it meant having less money?

1. YES → GO TO H69   5. NO

(268) H68. Would you like to spend more time working, in order to have more money, even if it meant spending less time with your (husband/wife) and child(ren)?

1. YES   5. NO

(271) H69. (RESPONDENT BOOKLET, PAGE 18)
Now I'd like you to read some questions starting with page 18 of your booklet and tell me the letter which best describes the way you feel. First, page 18, just tell me the letter.

ALL IN ALL, HOW SATISFIED WOULD YOU SAY YOU ARE WITH YOUR FAMILY LIFE?

5. EXTREMELY SATISFIED (A) 4. VERY SATISFIED (B) 3. SOMEWHAT SATISFIED (C) 2. NOT TOO SATISFIED (D)

76

ALL MARRIED R'S WITH NO CHILDREN UNDER 18

(268) H75. Would you like to spend less time working, so that you could spend more time with your (husband/wife), even if it meant having less money?

1. YES   GO TO H77
5. NO →

(268) H76. Would you like to spend more time working, in order to have more money, even if it meant spending less time with your (husband/wife)?

1. YES
5. NO

(245) H77. (RESPONDENT BOOKLET, PAGE 22)
Now, I'd like you to read the three questions starting with page 22 of your booklet and tell me the letter which best describes the way you feel. First, page 22, just tell me the letter.

HOW OFTEN DO YOU THINK ABOUT YOUR HUSBAND OR WIFE WHEN YOU'RE BUSY DOING OTHER THINGS?

5. ALWAYS (A)   4. OFTEN (B)   3. SOMETIMES (C)   2. RARELY (D)

(245) H78. (RESPONDENT BOOKLET, PAGE 23)
Then page 23, just give me the letter.

HOW MUCH DO YOU AGREE OR DISAGREE THAT THE MOST IMPORTANT THINGS THAT HAPPEN TO YOU INVOLVE YOUR MARRIAGE?

5. STRONGLY AGREE (A)   4. AGREE (B)   3. NEITHER AGREE NOR DISAGREE (NOT IN BOOKLET)   2. DISAGREE (C)   1. STRONGLY DISAGREE (D)

77

(269) H79. (RESPONDENT BOOKLET, PAGE 24)
And now turn to page 24.

AND ALL IN ALL, HOW SATISFIED WOULD YOU SAY YOU ARE WITH YOUR MARRIAGE?

5. EXTREMELY SATISFIED (A)   4. VERY SATISFIED (B)   3. SOMEWHAT SATISFIED (C)   2. NOT TOO SATISFIED (D)

TURN TO H85, PAGE 78

NON-MARRIED R'S WITH CHILDREN UNDER 18

(268) H80. Would you like to spend less time working, so that you could spend more time with your child(ren), even if it meant having less money?

1. YES   GO TO H82
5. NO →

(268) H81. Would you like to spend more time working, in order to have more money, even if it meant spending less time with your child(ren)?

1. YES
5. NO

(271) H82. (RESPONDENT BOOKLET, PAGE 25)
Now, I'd like you to read the three questions starting with page 25 of your booklet and tell me the letter which best describes the way you feel. First, page 25, just tell me the letter.

ALL IN ALL, HOW SATISFIED WOULD YOU SAY YOU ARE WITH YOUR FAMILY LIFE?

5. EXTREMELY SATISFIED (A)   4. VERY SATISFIED (B)   3. SOMEWHAT SATISFIED (C)   2. NOT TOO SATISFIED (D)

78

(245) H83. (RESPONDENT BOOKLET, PAGE 26)
Then, page 26, just the letter.

HOW OFTEN DO YOU THINK ABOUT YOUR CHILD OR CHILDREN WHEN YOU'RE BUSY DOING OTHER THINGS?

| 5. ALWAYS (A) | 4. OFTEN (B) | 3. SOMETIMES (C) | 2. RARELY (D) |

(246) H84. (RESPONDENT BOOKLET, PAGE 27)
Now, page 27.

HOW MUCH DO YOU AGREE OR DISAGREE THAT THE MOST IMPORTANT THINGS THAT HAPPEN TO YOU INVOLVE YOUR CHILD OR CHILDREN?

| 5. STRONGLY AGREE (A) | 4. AGREE (B) | 3. NEITHER AGREE NOR DISAGREE (NOT IN BOOKLET) | 2. DISAGREE (C) | 1. STRONGLY DISAGREE (D) |

ALL R'S EITHER MARRIED OR WITH CHILDREN UNDER 18

(264) H85. (RESPONDENT BOOKLET, PAGE 28)
How much do your job and your family life interfere with each other?

| 4. A LOT (A) | 3. SOMEWHAT (B) | 2. NOT TOO MUCH (C) | 1. NOT AT ALL (D) → TURN TO H87, PAGE 79 |

(265) H86. In what ways do they interfere with each other?

IF ONLY CONFLICT IN HOURS OR TIME IS MENTIONED: Any other ways?

_____

_____

_____

_____

79

(260) H87. (YELLOW SHOW CARD)
How much do you agree or disagree that it is much better for everyone involved if the man earns the money and the woman takes care of the home and children?

| 5. STRONGLY AGREE (A) | 4. AGREE (B) | 3. NEITHER AGREE NOR DISAGREE (NOT ON CARD) | 2. DISAGREE (C) | 1. STRONGLY DISAGREE (D) |

(267) H88. (YELLOW SHOW CARD)
How much do you agree or disagree that a mother who works outside the home can have just as good a relationship with her children as a mother who does not work?

| 5. STRONGLY AGREE (A) | 4. AGREE (B) | 3. NEITHER AGREE NOR DISAGREE (NOT ON CARD) | 2. DISAGREE (C) | 1. STRONGLY DISAGREE (D) |

Appendix B

Moderator Effects of Type of Worker and Family Life-Cycle Stage

Tables B.1 and B.2 present the moderator effects of type of worker and family life-cycle stage on the relationships between work schedule characteristics and family life. The tables include only those moderator effects that pass the first two basic tests, namely, the protected t and counting strategies. The data appear in this appendix rather than in the body of the text because the moderator effects fail the third test in the sequence, namely, the criterion of substantive significance. In short, the moderator effects reported here fail to display any interpretable pattern.

Type of Worker

Table B.1 indicates that, measured at the detailed level of separate terms in the regression equation, eight moderator effects based on type of worker clear the hurdles posed by the protected t and counting strategies. These eight effects involve three of the six dependent measures of family life (time with children, total work/family conflict, schedule conflict) and all three work schedule predictors (pattern of days worked, shift, number of hours worked each week). Type of worker moderates the effect of number of hours worked on parental time in two instances. Number of hours worked has a more negative effect on time in child care among dual-earner wives than among sole bread-winning husbands and, curiously, it has a positive effect among sole breadwinning wives.[1]

---

[1] Pleck (1981) reports a parallel analysis (with this dataset) comparing dual-earner wives with all employed husbands (i.e. sole breadwinning and dual-earner combined) with virtually identical results.

Type of worker also generates three moderator effects with shift as the predictor and total work/family conflict as the dependent variable. Night shift bears a negative relationship to total work/family inter- ference among female single parents compared to a positive relation- ship among sole breadwinning husbands. Rotating shift has a negative effect on conflict among sole breadwinning wives but a positive effect among sole breadwinning husbands. The residual category of other patterns of hours has a more positive effect among dual-earner wives than among sole breadwinning husbands.

Schedule conflict produces three moderator effects involving female single parents. Among the latter group, working variable days is positively related to schedule conflict though essentially unrelated among sole breadwinning husbands. Night shift has a negative effect on schedule conflict among female single parents but a positive rela- tionship among sole breadwinning husbands. Similarly, rotating shift has a negative relationship among female single parents compared to a positive relationship among sole breadwinning husbands. In sum, working variable days appears to create more scheduling conflicts for female single parents than for other groups including sole breadwin- ning husbands, yet nonday shifts appear to pose fewer schedule con- flicts for female single parents than for other groups.

Family Life-Cycle Stage

Family life-cycle stage generates nine moderator effects (again at the detailed level) that survive the protected t and counting strategies. Only two dependent variables (time on housework, hours conflict) and two predictors (shift, number of hours worked) are needed to represent the nine effects. According to Table B.2, in the case of time spent on housework, afternoon shift has a positive effect for all groups except childless married workers under forty-five among whom the effect is negative. Night shift has a more positive effect on time spent on housework among parents with an adolescent (aged thirteen to seven- teen) as their youngest child than among the childless under-forty-five group. Number of hours worked has a substantial negative effect on housework time among parents whose youngest child is in grade school (aged six to twelve) compared to the young childless group for whom there is scarcely any relationship.

The remaining three moderator effects concern number of hours worked and hours conflict. The effect of number of hours on hours conflict is more strongly positive for those under forty-five and childless than it is for parents of preschoolers or for those with an adolescent as their youngest child. Curiously, the effect is slightly negative for those married, childless, and forty-five or older.

TABLE B.1

Conditioning Effects of Type of Worker on Relationships between Work
Schedule Characteristics and Family Measures

Family Variables (Dep. Var.) Work Schedule Characteristics (Indep. Var.)	Effect of Work Schedule Characteristic When Type of Worker is:[a]						Increment to R²[b] Due to Interaction			
	Sole Breadwinning Husbands	Dual-Earner Husbands	Female Single Parents	Dual-Earner Wives	Sole Breadwinning Wives	Main Effect	Dual-Earner Husbands	Female Single Parents	Dual-Earner Wives	Sole Breadwinning Wives
Time in Child Care										
Number of Hours Worked	−.224	−.121	−.382	−.505*	1.230**	−.271	—	—	.0052	.0110
Total Conflict										
Night Shift	.568	.966	−.642*	.195	—[c]	.413**	—	.0048	—	—
Rotating Shift	.604	.526	−.188	.204	−.781*	.430**	—	—	—	.0050
Other Shift	.135	.046	.496	.525+	−.289	.204*	—	—	.0023	—
Schedule Conflict										
Variable Days	.045	.134	.673**	.006	.179	.133**	—	.0145	—	—
Night Shift	.283	.300	−.390**	.394	—[c]	.226**	—	.0075	—	—
Rotating Shift	.247	.251	−.691**	.164	−.139	.132*	—	.0108	—	—

+ p < .10.
* p < .05.
** p < .01.

[a]Significance levels of regression coefficients for interaction refer to comparisons between the category indicated and the referent category (sole breadwinning husbands).

[b]Increments to R² for significant interactions refer to comparisons between regression coefficients for the category indicated and the referent category (sole breadwinning husbands).

[c]No data are reported here because no sole breadwinning wives reported working the night shift.

TABLE B.2
Conditioning Effects of Family Life-Cycle Stage on Relationships between Work Schedule Characteristics and Family Measures

Family Variables (Dep. Var.) Work Schedule Characteristics (Indep. Var.)	Effect of Work Schedule Characteristic When Family Life-Cycle Stage is:[a]					Main Effect	Increment to R² Due to Interaction[b]			
	Childless, Under 45	Youngest Child Under 6	Youngest Child 6–12	Youngest Child 13–17	Childless, 45 or Older		Youngest Child Under 6	Youngest Child 6–12	Youngest Child 13–17	Childless, 45 or older
Time in Housework										
Afternoon Shift	-3.076	5.559+	5.386+	10.892*	16.234**	6.088**	.0022	.0016	.0026	.0069
Night Shift	7.679	2.758	2.938	32.972*	.899	4.182*	—	—	.0025	—
Number of Hours Worked	-.043	-.182	-.376**	-.164	-.169	-.452**	—	.0053	—	—
Hours Conflict										
Number of Hours Worked	.0263	.0126**	.0189	.0147+	-.0040**	.0095	.0063	—	.0029	.0141

+ p < .10.
* p < .05.
** p < .01.

[a]Significance levels of regression coefficients for interaction refer to comparisons between the category indicated and the referent category (childless, under 45).

[b]Increments to R² for significant interactions refer to comparisons between regression coefficients for the category indicated and the referent category (childless, under 45).

Appendix C

Additional Tables on Relationship between Husbands' and Wives' Starting and Ending Times

TABLE C.1

Wife's Shift by Husband's Shift (detailed form)[a]

Wife's Shift: Starting Time	Husband's Shift: Starting Time							
	3:30–6:59 am	7:00–7:59 am	8:00–8:59 am	9:00–11:59 am	Noon–5:59 pm	6:00 pm–3:29 am	Variable	All Shifts
3:30–6:59 am	5 / 9.6%	6 / 3.9%	2 / 1.6%	0 / 0%	1 / 4.2%	1 / 7.7%	4 / 4.3%	19 / 3.9%
7:00–7:59 am	10 / 19.2	37 / 24.2	20 / 16.0	10 / 30.3	4 / 16.7	1 / 7.7	18 / 19.6	100 / 20.3
8:00–8:59 am	21 / 40.4	44 / 28.8	55 / 44.0	7 / 21.2	6 / 25.0	5 / 38.5	25 / 27.2	163 / 33.1
9:00–11:59 am	1 / 1.9	23 / 15.0	17 / 13.6	9 / 27.3	5 / 20.8	1 / 7.7	14 / 15.2	70 / 14.2
Noon–5:59 pm	4 / 7.7	10 / 6.5	8 / 6.4	0 / 0	2 / 8.3	2 / 15.4	6 / 6.5	32 / 6.5
6:00 pm–3:29 am	2 / 3.8	7 / 4.6	3 / 2.4	0 / 0	0 / 0	1 / 7.7	2 / 2.2	15 / 3.0
Variable	9 / 17.3	26 / 17.0	20 / 16.0	7 / 21.2	6 / 25.0	2 / 15.4	23 / 25.0	93 / 18.9
All Shifts[b]	52 / 10.6	153 / 31.1	125 / 25.4	33 / 6.7	24 / 4.9	13 / 2.6	92 / 18.7	492 / 100

[a]Difference between husbands' and wives' distributions (comparison of row and column marginals): $X^2 = 46.1$, 6 df, $p < .001$; association between husbands' and wives' shift: $X^2 = 41.2$, 36 df, ns.

[b]Percents add up to 100 across this row; all other percents are column percents.

TABLE C.2
Wife's Ending Time by Husband's Ending Time

Wife's Ending Time	Husband's Ending Time						All Wives
	12:01 am–2:59 pm	3:00–3:59 pm	4:00–4:59 pm	5:00–5:59 pm	6:00–Midnight	Variable	
12:01 am–2:59 pm	6 / 14.6%	10 / 18.2%	15 / 13.4%	11 / 10.9%	16 / 18.0%	12 / 11.8%	70 / 14.0%
3:00–3:59 pm	8 / 19.5	14 / 25.5	22 / 19.6	18 / 17.8	14 / 15.7	18 / 17.6	94 / 18.8
4:00–4:59 pm	6 / 14.6	9 / 16.4	30 / 26.8	19 / 18.8	14 / 15.7	21 / 20.6	99 / 19.8
5:00–5:59 pm	7 / 17.1	14 / 25.5	15 / 13.4	21 / 20.8	17 / 19.1	13 / 12.7	87 / 17.4
6:00 pm–Midnight	4 / 9.8	1 / 1.8	10 / 8.9	13 / 12.9	12 / 13.5	11 / 10.8	51 / 10.2
Variable	10 / 24.4	7 / 12.7	20 / 17.9	19 / 18.8	16 / 18.0	27 / 26.5	99 / 19.8
All Husbands	41 / 8.2	55 / 11.0	112 / 22.4	101 / 20.2	89 / 17.8	102 / 20.4	500 / 100

[a]Difference between husbands' and wives' distributions (comparison of row and column marginals): $X^2 = 29.98$, 5 df, $p < .001$; association between husbands' and wives' ending time: $X^2 = 29.66$, 25 df, ns.
[b]Percents add up to 100 across this row; all other percents are column percents.

References

Aberle, D. F., and Naegele, K. "Middle-class fathers' occupational role and attitudes toward children." *American Journal of Orthopsychiatry* 22(1952): 366–378.

Agervold, M. "Shiftwork—A critical review." *Scandinavian Journal of Psychology* 17(1976): 181–188.

Aldous, J.; Osmond, M.; and Hicks, M. "Men's work and men's families." In *Contemporary theories about the family*, edited by W. Burr, R. Hill, I. Reiss, & F. I. Nye. New York: Free Press, 1979.

Andersen, J. E. *Treskiftsarbejde. En Socialmedicinsk Undersogelse.* Copenhagen: Socialforskningsinst, 1970. Cited in "Shiftwork—A critical review," by M. Agervold, *Scandinavian Journal of Psychology* 17(1976): 181–188.

Angell, R. C. *The family encounters the depression.* New York: Charles Scribner's Sons, 1936.

Bakke, E. W. *The unemployed worker: A study of the task of making a living without a job.* New Haven, CT: Yale University Press, 1940.

Banks, O. "Continuous shiftwork: The attitude of wives." *Occupational Psychology* 30(1956): 69–84.

Bast, G. H. *Ploegenarbeid in de Industry.* Arnhem: Contractgroepvoering Productiviteit Van Loghum Slaterus, 1960. Cited in *Health Consequences of Shiftwork*, by D. L. Tasto, M. J. Colligan, E. W. Skjei, & S. J. Polly. SRI Project URU-4426, March, 1978.

Blood, R. O., Jr., and Hamblin, R. L. "The effect of the wife's employment on the family power structure." *Social Forces* 36(1958): 347–352.

Blood, R. O., Jr., and Wolfe, D. M. *Husbands and Wives.* New York: Free Press, 1960.

Bohen, H. H., and Viveros-Long, A. *Balancing jobs and family life: Do flexible work schedules help?* Philadelphia: Temple University Press, 1981.

Brown, H. G. *Some effects of shiftwork on social and domestic life.* Hull University, Department of Economics and Commerce, 1959.

Carpentier, J., and Cazamian, P. *Night work.* Geneva: International Labour Organization, 1977.

Cavan, R. S., "Unemployment: Crisis of the common man." *Marriage and Family Living* 21(1959):139–146.

161

Chadwick-Jones, J. K. *Automation and behaviour: A social psychological study.* London: Wiley Interscience, 1969.

Clark, R. A., and Gecas, V. "The employed father in America: A role competition analysis." Paper presented at the Pacific Sociological Association, 1977.

Clark, R. A.; Nye, F. I.; and Gecas, V. "Husbands' work involvement and marital role performance." *Journal of Marriage and the Family* 40(1978): 9–21.

Cobb, S., and Kasl, S. V. *Termination: The consequences of job loss.* Dept. of Health, Education and Welfare (NIOSH), Publication No. 77-224. Washington, DC, 1977.

Cohen, J. B. "Multiple regression as a general data-analytic system." *Psychological Bulletin* 70(1968): 426–443.

Cohen, J., and Cohen, P. *Applied multiple regression/correlation analysis for the behavioral sciences.* Hillsdale, NJ: Lawrence Erlbaum Associates, 1975.

De la Mare, G., and Walker, J. "Factors influencing the choice of shift rotation." *Occupational Psychology* 42(1968): 1–21.

Dickinson, T. L., and Wijting, J. P. "An analysis of workers' attitudes toward the 4-day, 40-hour workweek." *Psychological Reports* 37(1975): 383–390.

Dizard, J. *Social change in the family.* Chicago: Community and Family Study Center, University of Chicago, 1968.

Drenth, P. J. D.; Hoolwerf, G.; and Thierry, H. "Psychological aspects of shiftwork." In *Personal goals and work design,* edited by P. Warr. London: Wiley, 1976.

Duncan, G., and Hill, C. R. "Modal choice in child care arrangements." In *Five Thousand American Families, Vol. 3,* edited by G. Duncan and J. Morgan. Ann Arbor, MI: Institute for Social Research, 1975.

Duncan, O. D. *Introduction to structural equation models.* New York: Academic Press, 1975.

Farkas, G. "Education, wage rates, and the division of labor between husband and wife." *Journal of Marriage and the Family* 38(1976): 473–484.

Feld, S. "Feelings of adjustment." In *The employed mother in America,* edited by F. I. Nye and L. W. Hoffman. Chicago: Rand McNally, 1963.

Ferree, M. M. "Working-class jobs: Housework and paid work as sources of satisfaction." *Social Problems* 23(1976): 431–441.

Freeman, R. B. "The work force of the future: An overview." In *Work in America,* edited by C. Kerr and J. M. Rosow. New York: Van Nostrand Reinhold, 1979.

Fullerton, H. N., Jr. "The 1995 labor force: A first look." *Monthly Labor Review* 103(12)(1980): 11–21.

Gerstl, J. E. "Leisure, taste, and occupational milieu." *Social Problems* 9 (1961): 56–68.

Greenhaus, J. H., and Kopelman, R. E. "Conflict between work and nonwork roles: Implications for the career planning process." *Human Resources Planning* 4(1981): 1–10.

Gronau, R. "The allocation of time of Israeli women." *Journal of Political Economy* 84(1976): S201–S220.

Guerin, J., and Durrmeyer, G. *Etude de la fatigue mentale industrielle.* Paris: Institut des Sciences Sociales du Travail, 1973. Cited in *Night work,* by J. Carpentier and P. Cazamian. Geneva: International Labour Organization, 1977.

Hayghe, H. "Husbands and wives as earners: An analysis of family data." *Monthly Labor Review* 104(2)(1981): 46–53.

Hedges, J. N. "The workweek in 1979: Fewer but longer workdays." *Monthly Labor Review* 103(8)(1980): 31–33.

Hedges, J., and Mellor, E. *10 million Americans work flexible schedules, 2 million work full time in 3 to 4½ days.* Dept. of Labor, Office of Information. Washington, DC, February, 1981.

Hedges, J., and Sekscenski, E. "Workers on late shifts in a changing economy." *Monthly Labor Review* 102(9)(1979): 14–22.

Hedges, J. N., and Taylor, D. E. "Recent trends in worktime: Hours edge downward." *Monthly Labor Review* 103(3)(1980): 3–11.

Heer, D. M. "Dominance and the working wife." *Social Forces* 36(1958): 341–347.

Hill, C. R., and Stafford, F. P. "Parental care of children: Time diary estimates of quantity, predictability and variety." *Journal of Human Resources* 15(1980): 219–239.

Hodge, B. J., and Tellier, R. D. "Employee reactions to the four-day week." *California Management Review* 18(1)(1975): 25–30.

Hofferth, S. L., and Moore, K. A. "Women's employment and marriage." In *The subtle revolution,* edited by R. E. Smith. Washington, DC: The Urban Institute, 1979.

Hoffman, L. W. "Maternal employment: 1979." *American Psychologist* 34 (1979): 859–865.

Hoffman, L. W., and Nye, F. I., eds. *Working mothers.* San Francisco: Jossey-Bass, 1974.

Hood, J., and Golden, S. "Beating time/making time: The impact of work scheduling on men's family roles." *The Family Coordinator* 28(1979): 575–582.

House, J. S. *Occupational stress and the mental and physical health of factory workers.* Research Report Series. Ann Arbor, MI: Institute for Social Research, 1980.

Kanter, R. M. *Work and family in the United States: A critical review and agenda for research and policy.* New York: Russell Sage Foundation, 1977.

———. "Work in a new America." *Daedalus* 107(1978): 47–78.

Keith, P. M., and Schafer, R. B. "Role strain and depression in two-job families." *Family Relations* 29(1980): 483–488.

Kemper, T. D., and Reichler, M. L. "Work integration, marital satisfaction, and conjugal power." *Human Relations* 29(1976): 929–944.

Kenny, M. T. "Public employee attitudes toward the four-day work week." *Public Personnel Management* 3(1974): 159–161.

Kerr, C., and Rosow, J. M., eds. *Work in America.* New York: Van Nostrand Reinhold, 1979.

Kish, L. "A procedure for objective respondent selection within the household." *Journal of the American Statistical Association* 44(1949): 380–387.

Kish, L., and Hess, I. *The Survey Research Center's national sample of dwellings.* Ann Arbor, MI: Institute for Social Research, 1965.

Kitagawa, E. M. "New life-styles: Marriage patterns, living arrangements, and fertility outside of marriage." *The Annals of the American Academy of Political and Social Science* 453(1981): 1–27.

Kohn, M. L. *Class and conformity.* Homewood, IL: Dorsey Press, 1969.

Kornhauser, A. *Mental health of the industrial worker.* New York: Wiley, 1965.

LaRocco, J. M.; House, J. S.; and French, J. R. P., Jr. "Social support, occupational stress, and health." *Journal of Health and Social Behavior* 21 (1980): 202–218.

Leibowitz, A. "Education and home production." *American Economic Review* 64(1974): 243–250.

Lein, L.; Durham, M.; Pratt, M.; Schudson, M.; Thomas, R.; and Weiss, H. *Final report: Work and family life.* National Institute of Education Project No. 3-3094. Wellesley, MA: Wellesley College Center for Research on Women, 1974.

Maklan, D. M. *The four-day workweek: blue collar adjustment to a nonconventional arrangement of work and leisure time.* New York: Praeger Publishers, 1977a.

———. "How blue-collar workers on 4-day workweeks use their time." *Monthly Labor Review* 100(8)(1977b): 18–26.

Mann, F., and Hoffman, L. *Automation and the worker.* New York: Henry Holt & Co., 1960.

Maurice, M. *Shift work.* Geneva: International Labor Office, 1975.

Maurice, M., and Monteil, C. *Vie quotidienne et horaires de travail: Enquête psychosociologique sur le travail en équipes successives.* Paris: Paris Institut des Sciences Sociales du Travail, 1965. Cited in *Health Consequences of Shift Work*, by D. L. Tasto, M. J. Colligan, E. W. Skjei, and S. J. Polly. SRI Project URU-4426, March, 1978.

Meissner, M.; Humphreys, E. W.; Meis, S. M.; and Scheu, W. J. "No exit for wives: Sexual division of labour and the cumulation of household demands." *Canadian Review of Sociology and Anthropology* 12(1975): 424–439.

Miller, A. R. "Changing work life patterns: A twenty-five year review." *The Annals of the American Academy of Political and Social Science* 435(1978): 83–101.

Miller, D., and Swanson, G. *The changing American parent.* New York: Wiley, 1958.

Moore, K. A., and Hofferth, S. L. "Women and their children." In *The subtle revolution*, edited by R. E. Smith. Washington, DC: The Urban Institute, 1979.

Mortimer, J. T. "Occupation-family linkages as perceived by men in the early stages of professional and managerial careers." In *Research in the interweave of social roles, Vol. 1: Women and men*, edited by H. Z. Lopata. Greenwich, CT: JAI Press, 1980.

Mott, P. E.; Mann, F. C.; McLoughlin, Q.; and Warwick, D. P. *Shift work: The social, psychological, and physical consequences.* Ann Arbor, MI: The University of Michigan Press, 1965.

Nollen, S. D., and Martin, V. H. *Alternative work schedules, Part 3: The compressed workweek.* New York: AMACOM, 1978.

Nord, W., and Costigan, R. "Worker adjustment to the four-day week: A longitudinal study." *Journal of Applied Psychology* 58(1973): 60–66.

Owen, J. "Worktime: The traditional workweek and its alternatives." In *Employment and Training Report of the President.* Dept. of Labor, Bureau of Statistics. Washington, DC, 1979.

Papanek, H. "Men, women, and work: Reflections on the two-person career." *American Journal of Sociology* 78(1975): 853–872.

Perrucci, C. C.; Potter, H. R.; and Rhoads, D. L. "Determinants of male family-role performance." *Psychology of Women Quarterly* 3(1978): 53–66.

Philips Factories. *Ploegenarbeid: Medissche, Maatschappelijke En Psychologische Gerolgen Van Ploegenarbeid.* Eindhoven, The Netherlands: Philips Factories, 1958. Cited in *Shift work: The social, psychological, and physical consequences*, by P. E. Mott, F. C. Mann, Q. McLoughlin, and D. P. Warwick. Ann Arbor, MI: The University of Michigan Press, 1965.

Piotrkowski, C. S., and Crits-Christoph, P. "Women's jobs and family adjustment." *Journal of Family Issues* 2(1981): 126–147.

Pleck, J. H. *Wives' employment, role demands, and adjustment: Final report to NIMH and NSF.* Wellesley, MA: Wellesley College Center for Research on Women, 1981.

———. "Husbands' paid work and family roles: Current research issues." In *Research on the interweave of social roles, Vol. 3: Families and jobs*, edited by H. Z. Lopata and J. H. Pleck. Greenwich, CT: JAI Press, in press.

Pleck, J. H., and Lang, L. *Men's family role: Its nature and consequences.* Wellesley, MA: Wellesley College Center for Research on Women, 1978.

Pleck, J. H.; Staines, G. L.; and Lang, L. *Work and family life: First reports on work-family interference and workers' formal childcare arrangements, from the 1977 Quality of Employment Survey.* Wellesley, MA: Wellesley College Center for Research on Women, 1978.

———. "Conflicts between work and family life." *Monthly Labor Review* 103(3)(1980): 29–32.

Quinn, R. P., and Associates. *Survey of Working Conditions: Final report on univariate and bivariate tables.* Document No. 2916-0001. Government Printing Office, Washington, DC, 1971.

Quinn, R. P., and Shepard, L. *The 1972–73 Quality of Employment Survey: Descriptive statistics, with comparison data from the 1969–70 Survey of Working Conditions.* Ann Arbor, MI: Survey Research Center, 1974.

Quinn, R. P., and Staines, G. L. *The 1977 Quality of Employment Survey.* Ann Arbor, MI: Survey Research Center, 1979.

Rainey, G. W., Jr., and Wolf, L. "Flex-time: Short-term benefits; long-term . . . ?" *Public Administration Review* 41(1981): 52–63.

Rapoport, R., and Rapoport, R. *Dual-career families.* London: Penguin, 1971.

Ridley, C. A. "Exploring the impact of work satisfaction and involvement on marital interaction when both partners are employed." *Journal of Marriage and the Family* 35(1973): 229–237.

Robinson, J. P. *How Americans use time: A social-psychological analysis of everyday behavior.* New York: Praeger, 1977.

Scanzoni, J. H. *Opportunity and the family: A study of the conjugal family in relation to the economic opportunity structure.* New York: Free Press, 1970.

Smith, R. E., ed. *The subtle revolution.* Washington, DC: The Urban Institute, 1979.

Stafford, R.; Backman, E.; and DiBona, P. "The division of labor among cohabiting and married couples." *Journal of Marriage and the Family* 39(1977): 43–57.

Staines, G. L. "Spillover versus compensation: A review of the literature on the relationship between work and nonwork." *Human Relations* 33(1980): 111–129.

Staines, G. L.; Pleck, J. H.; Shepard, L. J.; and O'Connor, P. "Wives' employment status and marital adjustment: Yet another look." *Psychology of Women Quarterly* 3(1978): 90–120.

Staines, G. L., and Quinn, R. P. "American workers evaluate the quality of their jobs." *Monthly Labor Review* 102(1)(1979): 3–12.

Steele, J. L., and Poor, R. "Work and leisure: The reactions of people at 4-day firms." In *4 days, 40 hours: Reporting a revolution in work and leisure,* edited by R. Poor. Cambridge, MA: Bursk & Poor, 1970.

Survey Research Center. "Types of living quarters defined." In *Interviewer's Manual,* rev. ed. Ann Arbor, MI: Institute for Social Research, 1976.

Swart, J. C. *A flexible approach to working hours.* New York: AMACOM, 1978.

Swerdloff, S. *The revised workweek: Results of a pilot study of 16 firms.* Dept. of Labor, Bureau of Statistics, Bull. 1846. Washington, DC, 1975.

Tasto, D. L.; Colligan, M. J.; Skjei, E. W.; and Polly, S. J. *Health consequences of shift work.* SRI Project URU-4426, March, 1978.

Ulich, E. "Zur Frage der Belastung des Arbeitenden Menschen durch Nacht und Schicktarbeit." *Psychologische Rundschau* 8(1957): 42–61. Cited in *Health consequences of shift work,* by D. L. Tasto, M. J. Colligan, E. W. Skjei, & S. J. Polly. SRI Project URU-4426, March, 1978.

Waldman, E.; Grossman, A. S.; Hayghe, H.; and Johnson, B. L. "Working mothers in the 1970's: A look at the statistics." *Monthly Labor Review* 102(10)(1979): 39–49.

Walker, J. *The human aspects of shiftwork.* London: Institute of Personnel Management, 1978.

Walker, K., and Woods, M. *Time use: A measure of household production of family goods and services.* Washington, DC: American Home Economics Association, 1976.

Walton, R. "Quality of work life activities: A research agenda." *Professional Psychology* 11(1980): 484–493.

Weitzman, M. S. "Finally the family." *The Annals of the American Academy of Political and Social Science* 435(1978): 61–82.

Winett, R.; Neale, M.; and Williams, K. "The effects of flexible work schedules on urban families with young children: Quasi-experimental, ecological studies." *American Journal of Community Psychology* 10(1982): 49–64.

Winett, R. A., and Neale, M. S. "Modifying settings as a strategy for permanent preventive behavior change: Flexible work schedules and family life as a case in point." In *Improving the long-term effects of psychotherapy,* edited by P. Karoly and J. J. Steffen. New York: Halsted Press, 1980a.

———. "Results of experimental study on flexitime and family life." *Monthly Labor Review* 103(11)(1980b): 29–32.

Wyatt, S., and Marriott, R. "Night work and shift changes." *British Journal of Industrial Medicine* 10(1953): 164–172.

Young, A. M. "Trends in educational attainment among workers in the 1970's." *Monthly Labor Review* 103(7)(1980): 44–47.

Young, M., and Willmott, P. *The symmetrical family.* New York: Pantheon, 1973.

Zalusky, J. "Shiftwork—A complex of problems." *AFL-CIO American Federationist,* May(1978): 1–6.